TASTES OF
WALES

GILLI DAVIES

BBC BOOKS

ACKNOWLEDGEMENTS

I should like to dedicate this book to my husband Alun and children Max, Augusta and Bonnie. Thank you all for your patience and fine appetites!

To the catering students of the Cardiff Institute of Higher Education under lecturer Les Hart, who tested the recipes, and in particular to Dawn Chiplin.

To Frances Roughley and Anne Churcher of Gelli Fawr Country House near Fishguard, for expertly cooking and assisting with the photographs.

To Taste of Wales and Welsh Lamb Enterprise for their financial support with the photographs.

To all the chefs, cooks and friends who have contributed the very best of their recipes to this book.

The television series *Tastes of Wales* is a BBC Wales production and was first shown on BB2 in Wales in Autumn 1990.
The series producer was Phil George, and the director was Richard Trayler-Smith.

Published by BBC Books,
a division of BBC Enterprises Limited,
Woodlands, 80 Wood Lane, London W12 0TT

First published 1990
© Gilli Davies 1990

Reprinted 1990 (twice) and 1991 (twice)

ISBN 0 563 36043 7

Photographs by Tim Imrie
Styling by Cathy Sinker
Home Economist Frances Roughley

Set in Palatino by Ace Filmsetting Ltd, Frome, Somerset
Text printing and binding in England by Clays Ltd, St Ives plc
Colour separations by Dot Gradations Ltd, Chelmsford
Colour printing in Great Britain by Lawrence Allen Ltd, Weston-super-Mare
Cover printed by Clays Ltd, St Ives plc

CONTENTS

INTRODUCTION

Croeso i Gymru – Welcome to Wales, principality of green hills and industrial valleys, rowdy rugby fans and rugged landscape, singing choirs and generous hospitality. But what about the food?

One wonders why a people so fiercely independent as the Welsh don't sing more about the virtues of their fine produce. Leeks, lamb and laverbread (edible seaweed) may be the familiar dishes of the Welsh diet, but there is much more to both traditional and modern Welsh food.

To me, Welsh food is home-grown quality fresh produce, and in this book and the television series, I aim to highlight how the best of it is incorporated in recipes of the past and the present.

Traditional Welsh dishes are a combination of the natural resources of the country blended with some skills and cooking methods brought by its invaders. They are based on oats, livestock and dairy products, with fresh supplements from the sea and the countryside.

The topography of Wales shows mainly uplands, with a quarter of its total area rising above 1000 ft. The well-conserved national parks – Snowdonia in the north, the Brecon Beacons in Powys, and Pembrokeshire to the west – account for 1600 square miles. There are good arable lowlands bordering its 750-mile coastline. Before the Industrial Revolution Wales was mainly pastoral and even now, outside the industrialised areas, it is a country of small farms.

A rugged landscape doesn't make for easy transport and, until recently, self-sufficiency was a code for survival for many of the more remote regions. Locally produced food shaped a spartan diet, but now that the mountains and rivers are no longer barriers, food from all over the world can be found in Wales.

Two thousand years ago the inhabitants of Wales were Celts and their cooking methods – boiling in a cauldron suspended over the fire and baking on a griddle – are still part of the Welsh cuisine.

The country was under Roman rule by AD 78 and, with their love of good food, the Romans appreciated the abundance of shellfish along the Welsh coast. This century has seen some of the original Roman vineyards replaced with new vines.

We have clear insight into the diet of the Welsh during the Middle Ages. Gerald Cambrensis, journeying through Wales with Archbishop Baldwin in 1188, noticed that most of the people lived on the produce of their herds and land: milk, butter, cheese and oats. In the eleventh century the Normans established earldoms on the Welsh border but the real conquest of Wales came in 1282 when Edward I of England defeated and killed the last native Welsh prince, Llywelyn ap Gruffud.

Owain Glyn Dwr led his countrymen in revolt against the English in 1400 and established a fervent nationalism in the Welsh which can be seen even in their diet. They refused to adopt the eating habits of the English nobility but stuck fiercely to their rural peasant diet.

In 1485 Henry Tudor, a Welshman, was crowned King of England and his son, Henry VIII, initiated the Act of Union between England and Wales. Was Wales brought into line? No, it was rebellious to the end! Nonconformity took a firm hold and the country became a stronghold of Methodism. This, combined with the poverty and harsh times of the Industrial Revolution, led the Welsh people to look to each other for support and in the rural communities many stores were shared.

The bacon pig is a good example. Every family reared one or two a year and between November and March the pigs were slaughtered one by one for the village by the travelling butcher. Each carcass would be divided and the fresh cuts shared amongst neighbours. The offal was used for faggots and brawn and the remainder cured for the forthcoming year.

Harvest time was also a community affair with help sought from neighbouring farms and a general atmosphere of conviviality. Dairy farms were prolific in the south-west and there was certainly bartering with butter, milk and cheeses. During these hard times the open hearth of the Welsh kitchen came into its own and the dishes that emerged are what we now regard as traditional Welsh cookery. The glowing embers of the robust open fire provided warmth and a good welcome as well as heat to cook nourishing, economical meals. Often you would find a ham, perhaps some fish or even cheese, tucked away in the chimney, where it was smoked to preserve it for later in the year.

During hard times oats could be served as often as three times a day, boiled in a cauldron – an essential Welsh cooking device – suspended over the fire. For breakfast there might be a bowl of *brwes*, crushed oatcake steeped in salt beef or bacon stock. Lunch, the main meal, would be *cawl*, a broth of salted bacon or beef boiled in the cauldron with potatoes and other vegetables. Often the meat and broth were eaten at different times to eke out the supplies. *Lobscow* was served in the counties of north Wales. Oatcakes would be served at teatime, especially in north Wales, and supper in south Wales might well be *llymru* or *sucan* – a sour oat-porridge.

The bakestone was the other vital cooking device and is still kept proudly by many Welsh households today. Originally this was a thin stone, later to be made of iron and called a *gradell, maen,* or *planc.* As well as scones, pancakes and Welsh cakes the housewife was a master at preparing flat-breads, deftly turned on the bakestone to cook through from both sides. The solid oven was perhaps lit only once a week, for baking day, and it was not until the arrival of the gas oven earlier this century that this weekly routine changed.

As for food in Wales today, traditional dishes survive only when they fit in with modern tastes and lives. How many of us manage to prepare a pot of *cawl* before we go to work in the morning? Who finds time to hover patiently over a warm bakestone turning Welsh cakes? Not many of us.

On the other hand, fresh brown trout cooked with herbs and wrapped in bacon, or lean lamb chops served with rowanberry jelly, sounds and tastes great.

Ease of travel and communications, fashion and the general improvement in cooking all influence the way we eat in Wales today, but none of these developments can contribute more to our food scene than fresh quality local food. So let's take a look at the produce Wales has to offer.

In the north fish arrives by the hour, round the clock, at Holyhead. This sophisticated, deep port has recently been modernised and deals with most of the seafish landed in Wales. (The majority of the fish goes straight to Europe where the price is better.) Smacks fish out of most of the small ports and the best fresh local fish is available at the shop on Penrhyn Port or through David Nigel Jones at the fish shop in Llandudno Junction.

The Menai Straits between Anglesey and the mainland is home to oyster beds as well as mussels, scallops and samphire. A horticultural industry is well established around Wrexham, where market gardeners are responding to the local demand for organic vegetables; local lamb and beef are of a high quality; dairy farmers produce their own yoghurts, soft and hard cheeses, and others make delicious, rich dairy ice cream.

The uplands of Wales specialise in rearing sheep. Welsh Lamb Enterprise, an organisation funded by the Welsh Development Agency, has encouraged lamb farmers to look to the future and to the standards they must attain in the single European market in 1992. Cross-breeding the Welsh mountain sheep has led to better-fleeced and more productive stock.

With beef, the story is the same. Many Welsh Blacks, one of the indigenous breeds of beef cattle of Wales, are now cross-bred with Continental breeds such as Limosin and Charolais to produce leaner, larger beasts. There is more profit for the farmer and the customer gets leaner beef, but I wonder if we are losing out on flavour.

The west and south-west coasts of Wales have seen a proliferation of small rural industries over the past 10 years – everything from organic farming to smoking venison. This fertile region has traditionally been the cereal-growing area and restored water mills again produce stone-ground flour as they did at the turn of the century.

Farmhouse cheeses include Acorn made from ewes' milk, Llanboidy made from Red Poll cows, Teifi, a gouda-type cheese, Ty'n Grug, a farmhouse Cheddar; and Caws Cenarth are again producing a traditional Caerphilly cheese. Organic farming for livestock, dairy and vegetables is a growth industry supplying the needs of local and distant restaurants.

Milford Haven has seen a steady decline since the war. Once the most important seaport in Wales, it s early morning quayside fish auction was a sight to be seen. Now it mainly handles larger vessels which land their catches straight into refrigerated lorries for transportation.

Scallops, mussels, cockles, winkles, oysters, crabs and lobsters are all caught around the Dyfed coast. Some find their way to local restaurants but many more go to the Continent in a large seawater tank. Is it that the Welsh housewife won't pay for home-grown quality produce, or is it that the catering trade won't lead the way?

The Teifi, Towy and Cleddau rivers bring fishermen in their shoals, tempted by the chance of catching a silvery salmon or *sewin* (sea trout) as they leap up the falls intent on returning to their spawning grounds. Brown trout run in the rivers, too.

In the south-east, the Usk and Wye tell the same fishing stories of men idling hours game fishing. Down on the estuaries the fishing is commercial, with netting licences costing a premium. The south-east also has fruit, market gardens, lamb and vineyards as well as large breweries and a tradition of good baking. Cardiff, the capital city of Wales, has a large ethnic population, stemming from the arrival of immigrants to work the extensive docks which were built on the coal wealth of the valleys. There is a constant supply of exotic foods and here more than anywhere in Wales the high quality and range of local foods might surprise the visitor.

One part of rural Welsh food that is seldom ignored by those who have time to spare is the gathering of wild harvests. Whether it's wild garlic in the spring, berries in the summer, wild fungi in the autumn or rabbits and pigeons during the winter, food for free always tastes better! It's a tough life though for those trying to make a living, like the cockle ladies scratching the sands at low tide, or the laver-gatherers off the Pembroke coast picking the slippery seaweed to make into laverbread.

Having established the source of good food in Wales, the next problem is distributing it. This has been the biggest headache for so many restaurants that want to serve Welsh food.

Luckily, enterprising groups have set up small delivery services and it is not unusual to order smoked turkey from Dyfed only to find that your ice cream arrives on the same van!

Producers and suppliers are getting together and one of the best services open to restaurants is the travelling Welsh cheese board, where a variety of different Welsh cheeses can be ordered at a time.

From Abergavenny, Vin Sullivan now runs one of the premier supply businesses in the UK. If you live on the coast you can ask him for Welsh pheasants; if you live inland, he will supply sea and shellfish.

The Wales Tourist Board promotes all outlets and at last the good news about food in Wales is stretching over the borders. Food producers enjoy good support and advice from the Welsh Development Agency and a company called 'A Taste of Wales' has been set up recently to look after the needs and standards of the catering trade. So the Welsh food scene is looking particularly healthy, as we set out to demonstrate. If you haven't eaten out in Wales, it is high time you did!

Many fine chefs were known to us when we chose those featured in the series, and our choice was not easy. However, the series was produce-led and within each programme it was important to find a cook who used local produce and adapted his or her own personal talent to show it at its best.

FIRST COURSES

The traditional Welsh first course is a bowl of soup. Not just any bowl of soup, but the delicious broth in which lamb or beef for a main course has been cooked together with a selection of vegetables and herbs. This then is Welsh *cawl*. Altogether a very economical, tasty and satisfying way to eat, especially if you have been out working hard in the fields all day.

Today, though, with our sedentary lifestyle, and excess of rich ingredients, we need to rein in at the beginning of a good meal for fear of not running the course to the puddings.

But isn't the first course often the most pleasing thing on the menu? I find there is a great temptation to have two and forget about the main course.

Nowhere is this more true than at Plas Bodegroes, where the skilled hand of Chris Chown offers simply too many goodies on the first page of his menu. Chris has chosen to run his restaurant in a location where he is literally spoilt for choice when it comes to ingredients. On the Lleyn Peninsula he is within easy reach of scallops, crab and lobster from Cardigan Bay, mussels and oysters from the Menai Straits, to say nothing of edible seaweeds along the west coast of Wales.

Demanding on his suppliers, Chris aims to serve the very best of fresh local ingredients, and it seems that his challenge is being met. Organic vegetables are now produced in the region and local game as well as excellent meat and poultry.

No one is better off for game than Eileen Havard at the Griffin Inn at Llyswen in Powys; she doesn't have to rely on suppliers, locals simply bring their catch into the bar where the publican, Richard Stockton, is only too pleased to accept it. What better way to start a meal in the winter than with a bowl of steaming game soup?

Who'd be a cockle-gatherer on a cold windy day, dashing down to scrape the sand flats as the tide goes out and expose those tasty molluscs? Back-breaking work, but if it means a bagful of fresh boiled cockles, sprinkled with pepper and a dash of vinegar, then it's worth the toil!

Mussels make a fine first course, and Kim and Val Mold run their Mytti Mussel business out of Penrhyn Bay in the north so successfully that they now export as many as 3–4000 tons of mussels a year, many of them to France.

Why to France? Because the French love Kim's clean, scrubbed mussels and they are willing to pay a realistic price for them.

Tons of tasty little Welsh queen scallops take the same route to France, Spain and Portugal from Wilsons of Holyhead. In fact it seems that the very best of Welsh shellfish, as well as our sea fish, leaves these shores almost as soon as it is landed.

Lobsters are collected daily along the west coast and transported live in seawater tanks in a *vivier* lorry direct to the Continent. Who can blame the fishermen, though, if it means a better regular price?

Let's take to the hedgerows too while looking for a first course. Margaret Rees will stimulate our tastebuds with a bowl of her elderflower and rhubarb soup, an unusual combination of flavours. Hazelnut pâté, a recipe from Jan Mifsud at the Lake Hotel in Llangamarch Wells, is delicious and if we really feel like an escape from the madding crowd let's head for the sand flats off the Dyfed coast and gather some samphire and laverbread to whet our appetites.

ELDERFLOWER AND RHUBARB SOUP

Over the past nine years customers at Margaret Rees' Cobblers Restaurant in Llandybie, Dyfed, have enjoyed an assortment of sophisticated country dishes such as this Elderflower and Rhubarb Soup.
Margaret also serves this soup as a sauce with lamb, pork, salmon or our Welsh sea trout, sewin. She suggests that alternative flavourings to add to the soup could be a few pieces of preserved ginger or fresh angelica stems.
The soup should be cooked in a stainless steel or glass saucepan to avoid the metallic taste which sometimes appears when the acid in the rhubarb reacts with aluminium.

SERVES 4

1 oz (25 g) butter
1 large onion, diced
2 lb (1 kg) rhubarb, diced

1½ pints (900 ml) elderflower champagne
the zest and juice of 1 orange

1 Melt the butter in a saucepan and fry the onion and rhubarb gently for 10 minutes. Add the elderflower champagne and continue to cook gently for a further 10–15 minutes.

2 Add the orange zest and juice and liquidise. Strain if the rhubarb is at all stringy.

3 If the consistency is too heavy for a soup add more liquid in the form of water, wine or even milk if a creamy consistency is desired.

4 This soup can be served warm or chilled; garnish with a swirl of cream.

COCKLE CAKES WITH FRESH TOMATO SAUCE

Selwyn Lynch, from Penclawdd on the Gower Peninsula, has been gathering cockles for the past 50 years and still enjoys a handful of them freshly boiled, dusted with vinegar and pepper, at any time of the day.
A cockle-gatherer's life is not an easy one. Come rain or shine Selwyn returns from the estuary at low tide where he has scratched the cockles from under the sand and his hands are red raw from the cold.
He sells his catch from his vans, and tells how in Swansea they like their cockles pan-fried with bacon and crisp breadcrumbs whilst in the Gwendraeth valley poor man's tart is popular – when cockles are stirred into a thick white sauce and served in a pastry case. Visitors to Wales may well be offered cockles fried with bacon and laverbread for breakfast. Delicious! I suggest serving a sharp tomato and garlic sauce with these crisp cockle cakes.

SERVES 4

4 oz (100 g) self-raising flour
4 oz (100 g) oatmeal (medium)
2 eggs
10 fl oz (300 ml) milk
salt and freshly ground black pepper
8 oz (225 g) cockles, freshly boiled
oil for frying

For the sauce:
1 tablespoon olive oil
1 medium onion, chopped
2 cloves garlic, crushed
1 tablespoon flour
1 lb (450 g) fresh tomatoes or 1 × 14 oz (400 g) tin tomatoes
1 teaspoon tomato purée
1 teaspoon oregano
1 tablespoon dry red or white wine
salt, freshly ground black pepper and a pinch of sugar

1 Make a batter with the flour, oatmeal, eggs, milk and seasoning and leave it to thicken for half an hour.

2 Stir the cockles into the batter.

3 Heat the oil in a deep pan and drop tablespoonfuls of the mixture into the hot oil. Fry for about 2 minutes, until crisp and golden.

4 Drain the cockles on kitchen paper and serve at once with warm tomato and garlic sauce.

The sauce:

5   Heat the oil in a small saucepan and sweat the onion gently for 5 minutes so that it softens but does not brown. Turn the heat up a little and add the crushed garlic. Continue to fry until the onion and garlic turn a golden brown

6   Stir in the flour and cook through for a minute. Stir in the tomatoes, purée, herbs, wine and seasoning and simmer over gentle heat for 10 minutes, stirring to break up the tomatoes.

7   Sieve the sauce and serve separately with the cockle fritters.

MUSHROOM AND HAZELNUT PÂTÉ

This recipe was given to me by Jan Mifsud at the Lake Hotel in Llangamarch Wells, who prepares it frequently using a microwave oven. Both mushrooms and hazelnuts grow in the magnificent grounds of the hotel and if any unusual edible mushrooms pop up during the night, such as chanterelles or cèpes, they find themselves arranged in a layer through the middle of the pâté.

SERVES 4

2 oz (50 g) butter
1 medium-sized onion, chopped
1 lb (450 g) mushrooms (flat field ones, if possible), chopped
¼ teaspoon grated nutmeg
the grated rind of ½ lemon
salt and pepper

4 oz (100 g) wholemeal breadcrumbs
2 oz (50 g) hazelnuts, toasted and roughly chopped

A 1 lb (450 g) loaf tin or suitable pâté dish lined with oiled greaseproof paper

1   Melt the butter in a saucepan or microwave dish. Add the onion and mushrooms and cook gently together, covered, until soft.

2   Transfer to a food processor. Add the nutmeg, lemon rind, seasoning, breadcrumbs and hazelnuts. Chop till the right consistency is reached – not too fine but not so coarse that the hazelnuts are left in large pieces.

3   Spread the pâté into the lined tin or dish, smooth the top and leave in the fridge to firm.

4   Turn the pâté out and serve in slices with warm toast.

VEGETABLES IN BEER BATTER

When you mix self-raising flour with beer the yeast reacts to give a wonderful light and fluffy batter which tastes particularly good when used to coat crisp vegetables. Peter Adams at the Rock and Fountain Inn in Brynmawr near Abergavenny gave me this idea. He serves these vegetable beignets with a garlic-flavoured mayonnaise, and I like to add a handful of chopped sorrel if I can find it. You could use any combination of crisp vegetables.

SERVES 4

4 oz (100 g) self-raising flour
a pinch of salt
¼ pint (150 ml) best bitter
4 oz (100 g) cauliflower (cut into florets)
4 oz (100 g) snow peas or mange-tout
1 large carrot, cut into matchsticks
2 oz (50 g) whole button mushrooms
2 oz (50 g) baby corn

For the mayonnaise:
4 tablespoons home-made or best quality bought mayonnaise mixed with 1 crushed clove of garlic and 1 tablespoon chopped sorrel

1 Prepare the beer batter by sieving the flour into a bowl, add a pinch of salt and blend in the beer slowly until the mixture reaches the consistency of double cream. Cover and leave in a warm place while you prepare the vegetables (about 10 minutes).

2 Blanch the cauliflower and snow peas by covering with cold water in a saucepan and bringing to the boil. Drain and rinse under cold running water.

3 Pat dry and coat the cauliflower, snow peas, carrots, mushrooms and baby corn with batter. Deep-fry quickly in hot oil, until golden brown.

GRIFFIN INN GAME SOUP

With the crisp autumn winds blowing rain-filled clouds across the Brecon Beacons, you can imagine how weary and cold the shooting party must be as they return to the Griffin Inn in the late afternoon. Not for long, though. As the chatter begins in the cosy bar, by the roaring wood fire, tired bodies begin to revive under the spell of Eileen Havard's Game Soup. Vegetables, diced bacon and a little spicy chilli powder are key ingredients, with pasta shells to add body and a selection of game – but not too much hare or grouse, suggests Eileen, in case they overpower the subtle flavour.

SERVES AT LEAST 8 VERY HUNGRY HUNTERS!

2 oz (50 g) butter
1 medium onion, diced
4 oz (100 g) carrots, peeled and diced
1 medium leek, sliced
2 oz (50 g) celery, sliced
4 oz (100 g) swede, diced
4 oz (100 g) cauliflower, broken into
  florets
1 clove garlic, crushed
2 rashers streaky bacon, diced
½ teaspoon chilli powder

salt and freshly ground black pepper
6 pints (3.4 litres) game or chicken stock
2 oz (50 g) pasta shells
8 oz (225 g) cooked game (pheasant, hare,
  rabbit, partridge, grouse, pigeon)
1 tablespoon Worcestershire sauce
1 tablespoon port or sweet sherry
  (optional)
4 teaspoons cornflour mixed with 4
  tablespoons water to thicken (optional)

1   Melt the butter in a large saucepan and gently fry the vegetables, garlic and bacon for 5 minutes.

2   Add the chilli powder, salt and pepper and pour in the game or chicken stock and bring to the boil.

3   Add the pasta and simmer until it is almost tender. Add the cooked game and cook for another minute or two to heat right through.

4   Correct the seasoning, add Worcestershire sauce and sherry to taste. Thicken slightly with cornflour if you wish.

5   Serve with warm bread rolls and butter.

MUSSELS IN A SAVOURY CHOUX PASTRY CASE

Kim Mold's mussels, which sell under the label Mytti Mussel, from Port Penrhyn on the Menai Straits, are so good that the French buy a great many of them. Cunning people, the French!
You can buy mussels live by the pint, cooked, shelled or frozen, so even if you don't live near mussel beds there's no excuse to avoid these tasty inexpensive molluscs.

SERVES 6

For the pastry:
¼ pint (150 ml) water
2 oz (50 g) butter
salt and pepper
3 oz (75 g) flour
2 eggs
¼ teaspoon English mustard

4 lb (1.75 kg) fresh mussels in their shells
   or 12 oz (350 g) shelled cooked mussels

1 large onion, chopped
1 clove garlic, chopped
sprigs of fresh parsley
1 tablespoon crushed coriander seeds
8 fl oz (250 ml) dry white wine
4 fl oz (120 ml) water
freshly ground black pepper
¼ pint (150 ml) double cream
1 tablespoon finely chopped parsley

1   Pre-heat the oven to gas mark 7, 425°F (220°C).

2   Prepare the pastry by placing the water, butter, salt and pepper in a saucepan and bring to the boil to melt the butter. Take off the heat and add all the sifted flour at once. Stir until the mixture is smooth and leaves the sides of the pan. Cool for 5–10 minutes.

3   Add the eggs one at a time, beating hard until the mixture is smooth and shiny and keeping its shape. Add the mustard.

4   Either use a 10 inch (25 cm) flan dish or 6 large ramekins or individual heatproof serving dishes and spread a layer of pastry around the edge, about ½ inch (1 cm) thick.

5   Scrub the mussel shells and put them in a large saucepan. Add the onion, garlic, parsley, coriander, wine, water and seasoning.

6   Cover and cook over a high heat until the shells open, shaking the pan from time to time – this takes about 5 minutes. Take care not to overcook the mussels or they will toughen. Discard any shells that refuse to open.

7   Strain the liquid from the mussels into a small pan and boil well to reduce to about a wineglassful. (If you are using cooked shelled mussels, simply combine the onion, garlic, parsley, coriander, wine, water and seasoning and boil to reduce, then strain.)

8   Add the cream and chopped parsley, stir to blend, then cool. Shell the mussels and add them to the cream sauce.

9   Meanwhile, bake the pastry in a hot oven for 10–15 minutes or until risen and golden brown and allow another 10 minutes for the larger flan dish to cook.

10   Reheat the mussels in the sauce and spoon into the middle of the cooked pastry. Serve at once.

SPICED LEEK AND POTATO SOUP

The national emblem, worn in lapels on St David's Day, the leek holds a place of high esteem with the Welsh.
In this soup, the combination of leeks and potatoes is used to make either a warming winter soup or a sophisticated chilled soup for a hot summer's day.

SERVES 4

1 oz (25 g) butter or margarine	1 teaspoon mild curry paste
4 medium-sized leeks, trimmed, washed and chopped	1 teaspoon coriander seeds, freshly ground
2 medium-sized potatoes, peeled and chopped	1 pint (600 ml) chicken stock
	4 tablespoons single cream
	chopped fresh coriander leaves

1   Melt the butter in a medium-sized saucepan and fry the vegetables with the curry paste and coriander seeds for 3–4 minutes, until they start to soften and colour.

2   Add the chicken stock and bring to the boil. Cover and simmer for 30 minutes or until the vegetables are soft.

3   Purée the soup and sieve for a really fine texture.

4   Adjust seasoning, cover and chill for 2 hours, preferably overnight.

5   Just before serving, swirl the cream on top of the soup as a garnish with the fresh coriander.

MOUSSELINE OF SCALLOP, CRAB AND LAVERBREAD WITH CRAB SAUCE

Sensational, this one: as you cut into your creamy mousseline, out pours a thick green laverbread sauce and, as if this wasn't enough, the sauce surrounding the mousseline tastes of crab! Altogether a classy dish and Chris Chown points out that this recipe is not for beginners. He also suggests that crab meat can be substituted for a whole crab, but it is then difficult to make the sauce (no crab stock).

King scallops can be used but they are twice the price of queen scallops. (They are also much larger so only one should be reserved for each mousse and cut into three.) Chris uses tinned Drangway laverbread and this makes a good substitute if you are unable to get a fresh supply from your fishmonger.

Scallops are best in the autumn and spring and Chris recommends they should be bought in their shells to ensure that they are fresh. It is a common trick to pump scallops with water and if either watery or frozen scallops are used, the mousse is likely to fall to bits.

This mousse is not cheap to make, working out at slightly more than £1 per portion.

SERVES 8 AS A STARTER

1 lb (450 g) crab
½ in (1 cm) fresh ginger, finely chopped
salt and pepper
1 small onion, chopped
½ stick celery, chopped
1 clove garlic, chopped
1 oz (25 g) butter
2 fl oz (50 ml) medium sherry
1 teaspoon tomato purée
1 bayleaf

For the mousse:
7 lb (3 kg) queen scallops in shells or 1 lb (450 g) fresh shelled queen scallops (approx 60 scallops)

salt and pepper
1 egg
7 fl oz (200 ml) double cream, chilled
4 oz (100 g) laverbread

For the sauce:
3½ fl oz (100 ml) white wine
3½ fl oz (100 ml) double cream
1 fl oz (25 ml) medium sherry
2½ oz (65 g) butter
seasoning

1   Pre-heat the oven to gas mark 3, 325°F (160°C).

2   Boil the crab for 10 minutes in salted water. Plunge immediately into a bowl of iced water to cool as quickly as possible.

3   Shell the crab and discard the stomach and dead man's fingers. Remove both the white and brown meat.

4 Reserve half the brown meat. Mix the other half with all the white meat and the ginger. Season and reserve.

5 Smash all the crab shell pieces in an 8inch (20 cm) saucepan. Add the onion, celery, garlic and butter and sweat until they begin to brown. Add the sherry, the tomato purée and the bayleaf; cover the pan for a minute. Pour in 1 pint (600 ml) water and simmer for 1 hour.

The mousse:

6 Select 24 nice scallops. Detach the roes and reserve.

7 You should have approximately 9 oz (250 g) white scallop meat. Put this in a food processor bowl, sprinkle with a little salt and chill for 30 minutes. Add the egg and purée for 60 seconds, gradually adding ¾ of the well-chilled cream. Rub through a fine sieve. Add pepper. Poach a small amount in simmering water to test consistency; if it is very firm, add a little more chilled cream. Test again until it is light. (Remember, laverbread is very salty.)

8 Butter 8 × 4 fl oz (120 ml) timbale moulds or ramekins. Divide the mousse between them and form a well in the centre. Place a teaspoon of laverbread and then a teaspoon of the reserved mixed crabmeats in each. Push in the reserved scallop roes and chill.

The sauce:

9 Strain the stock into a clean pan; add the wine and cream and reduce the quantity by half (this will take about 20 minutes).

10 Stir in the reserved brown crabmeat and sherry. Bring back to the boil, then sieve into a clean pan.

11 Whisk in 2 oz (50 g) butter and reheat, checking seasoning.

12 Steam the mousselines for 8 minutes or cook them in a *bain marie* in the oven for 10–12 minutes, until slightly risen and firm.

13 Heat a small non-stick frying-pan until very hot; toss in the scallops and remaining butter and sauté until brown on both sides.

14 Turn the mousselines out on to individual plates, surround with sauce and three sautéed scallops each.

LYNDA'S CAWL

Cawl, the 'all-in-stew' soup, was at one time the staple diet of many Welsh families, the meat from the pot served at one meal with the broth kept overnight for the next day. Many of the older generation remember it with affection and a few of the younger generation still make it. With our modern healthy eating habits the recipe for cawl has seen changes over the years; the meat is leaner, the vegetables more abundant and the broth served well skimmed of fat.

This recipe given to me by Lynda Kettle, who runs a small hotel at her Ty'n Rhos Farm in Llandeiniolen outside Bangor, is deliciously filling and full of assorted flavours. Being a perfectionist, Lynda always makes her own stock but as a short cut you could use the fresh stock now available from some supermarkets.

One diehard habit that I encourage is to float a few marigold petals on the top of the cawl just before serving.

SERVES 4

For brown stock:

1 onion, skin left on
2 sticks celery, chopped
1 large carrot, chopped
1 large leek, chopped

½ shoulder Welsh lamb
1½ tablespoons barley, split peas or
  lentils (optional)

pinch of cloves
1 bayleaf
3 large carrots, peeled and diced
1 large onion, diced
1 parsnip or turnip, diced
2 large leeks, chopped
1 stick celery, chopped
salt and pepper
lots of freshly chopped parsley

1 Take the meat off the bone and trim the fat. Cut the meat into very small dice or use a food processor.

Brown stock:

2 Put the bones in a roasting tin and brown in the oven with the trimmings for 30 minutes.

3 Remove the bones to a large saucepan, drain off most of the juices and sauté the stock vegetables in the tin for 10 minutes.

4 Add them to the bones, cover with plenty of water and simmer gently for 3½ hours (or pressure cook for 20 minutes). Strain the stock, cool and skim. Measure and if necessary boil down to 4 pints (2.25 litres).

5 Sauté the diced lamb in a non-stick pan over a high heat and then add it to the reduced stock with the barley and lentils, cloves and bayleaf. Simmer for 40 minutes.

6   Heat some of the residual lamb fat from the roasted bones and quickly sauté the chopped vegetables, reserving some of the leeks. Drain and add to the simmering lamb and stock, season and cook for a further 30 minutes. Add remaining leeks and cook for another 10 minutes.

7   Serve with a liberal scattering of marigold petals or parsley and lots of crusty bread.

LAVERBREAD NUGGETS WITH BACON AND OATMEAL

'Ah! call us not Weeds, but Flowers of the Sea' – from a Victorian seaweed picture. Welshman's caviar is how Richard Burton described laverbread, and this dark green gelatinous seaweed does have rather exotic appeal. Gathered off the rocks around the Pembrokeshire coast, the laver or **Porphyra** *umbilicalis is washed well, boiled for many hours, then minced to be sold as a pulp. Rich in minerals, it has always been popular along the south coast of Wales and even today vans travel daily to the markets in the mining valleys selling laverbread.*
Traditionally served for breakfast tossed in oatmeal and fried with bacon, I suggest laverbread deserves a place on the dinner table too, and this recipe combines those same ingredients to make crisp nuggets.
Laverbread is available in tins, so there is no excuse to avoid this luxury!

MAKES ABOUT 24

4 slices streaky smoked bacon   *medium oatmeal*
8 oz (225 g) pulped laverbread   *salt and freshly ground black pepper*

1   Dice the bacon and dry fry it so that it is crisp and brown. Stir it into the laverbread.

2   Add enough oatmeal to the bacon fat in the frying-pan to make a firm dough, season with plenty of pepper and a little salt, then roll the mixture into walnut-sized balls.

3   Flatten them slightly, then fry gently in the bacon fat until crisp and brown on both sides.

4   Serve the laverbread nuggets hot from the pan with a sharp sauce such as Fresh Tomato Sauce on page 12 or a slice of lemon.

TROUT AND SORREL TERRINE

In an ideal world I would like to eat a fresh brown trout from an unpolluted Welsh river, but failing that I think well-farmed rainbow trout makes a good second best. Fillets of rainbow trout are reasonably priced and I find them convenient when preparing a terrine of trout. Their pretty pink colour and delicate flavour blend well with the sorrel cream and make this an attractive dish.
The texture and flavour improve over a couple of days, so make it ahead of time and leave it to firm up in the fridge.

SERVES 4

12 large sorrel leaves (alternatively use
  fresh spinach)
15 oz (425 g) half fat cream cheese

1 egg yolk
salt and pepper
3 good sized fillets of pink rainbow trout

1 Pre-heat the oven to gas mark 4, 350°F (180°C).

2 Take a 1 pint (600 ml) mould, any heat-proof dish will do, and arrange half of the sorrel leaves over the base and around the sides.

3 Chop the remaining sorrel leaves finely and blend with the cream cheese. Add the egg yolk and season well with salt and pepper. (A food processor ruins the texture – so do this by hand.)

4 Lay fillets of trout, skin side down, on a chopping board. Using a sharp knife, separate the flesh from the skin. Run your finger over the trout fillets to see if there are any tiny bones and remove these with a pair of tweezers.

5 Lay half the fish fillets over the sorrel leaves and cover them with half the cream cheese mixture. Arrange the remaining trout on top of the cheese and finish with the last of the cream cheese. Cover the terrine with foil or clingfilm.

6 Bake the terrine in a larger dish, half full of water, for 30 minutes in the oven or 10 minutes in the microwave.

I serve this trout and sorrel terrine in slices surrounded by a Vodka Tomato Sauce: Mix thick tomato pulp with a little vodka and Worcestershire sauce.

LEEK AND GOAT'S CHEESE PARCELS

A mature Crottin de Chavignol, *the tiny salted French goat's cheeses, have a
definite tang, and are rather an acquired taste. But soft fresh Welsh goat's cheese is
quite a different thing. Look out for Tony Craske's Pant Ysgawn.
Fresh goat's cheese is as mild as cream cheese and infinitely less fattening. It is sold
in most supermarkets and comes in small 4 oz tub-shaped packs, either plain, rolled
in herbs, or covered with crushed peppercorns. For this recipe I have used plain
goat's cheese and mixed it with chopped walnuts before rolling it into a leek.
The honey vinaigrette adds just a little sweetness to the dish.*

SERVES 4

2 medium-sized leeks
4 oz (100 g) fresh goat's cheese
2 oz (50 g) walnuts, chopped
1 oz (25 g) raisins, soaked in sherry for
    30 minutes

For the dressing:
3 tablespoons walnut oil
1 tablespoon white wine vinegar
1 teaspoon runny honey
salt and freshly ground black pepper

1   Discard the tough outer skins of the leeks and wash them under
cold running water. Keep them whole and plunge them into a large
saucepan of boiling water; boil for 8 minutes, drain and immediately
run under the cold tap. This will cool them quickly and also maintain
the bright green colour.

2   Peel the layers off the leeks, tearing them as little as possible.
Reserve the best 8 layers and chop the remainder finely.

3   Mix the chopped leeks, goat's cheese, walnuts and raisins and
divide the mixture into 4 portions.

4   Wrap each portion in two leek layers, making a parcel shape.
Arrange the leek parcels on a serving dish.

5   Put all the ingredients for the dressing into a wide-topped jam jar.
Shake well to blend.

6   Spoon some dressing over each parcel.

SALMON BAKED IN FILO WITH SAMPHIRE

Standing on the shore at the mouth of the Teifi River just outside Cardigan I remember feeling full of anticipation as the team of four netsmen pulled in their long seine net. The season is short, rules are very strict and licences hard to obtain for this special form of fishing, but there is a great desire for the netsmen to maintain the tradition and they still try to catch the salmon as they leave the sea and head upriver to their native spawning grounds.
As with all fish there is a need to keep it moist while cooking and by wrapping the salmon in filo pastry not only does the flesh stay moist but all the flavour is sealed in too.
The bright green samphire adds colour and texture to this fine dish.

SERVES 4

4 sheets filo pastry, approx 12 × 9 in (30 × 23 cm)
approx 4 oz (100 g) melted butter
12 oz (350 g) fresh salmon, without bones
4 teaspoons fromage frais
4 sprigs lemon balm or 4 slices fresh lemon
salt and freshly ground black pepper

For the Samphire Sauce:
8 oz (225 g) fresh samphire
1 oz (25 g) unsalted butter
3½ fl oz (100 ml) dry white wine
freshly ground black pepper

1   Heat the oven to gas mark 8, 450°F (230°C).

2   Divide the salmon into 4 pieces, though it doesn't matter if you end up with quite a few small lumps of fish.

3   Take a sheet of filo pastry and speedily paint half of it with melted butter, folding the other half over the painted surface. Paint the top of the folded-over half and place a quarter of the salmon in the centre of each square.

4   Add a teaspoon of fromage frais, a sprig of lemon balm or a slice of fresh lemon and seasoning. Fold the pastry over to make a parcel and coat the outside with melted butter.

5   Repeat this for all 4 sheets of filo.

6   Put the prepared parcels in a baking tin and cook for 8–10 minutes; they will be cooked when the pastry is crisp and golden.

7   For the sauce, first pick over the samphire, carefully removing any brown ends or woody pieces.

8   Put it in a saucepan, cover with cold water and bring to the boil.

9   Then strain and rinse immediately under the cold tap to preserve the lovely bright green colour.

10   Melt the butter in a frying-pan and toss the samphire into it, stirring well until all the samphire is coated with the butter.

11   Pour in the wine and season well with black pepper. Bring to the boil and allow to simmer for 3 minutes.

12   Keep the sauce in a warm place until needed.

13   To serve, place one salmon parcel on each plate and spoon the samphire around the outside in a circle. Pour the pan juices carefully over the samphire and serve immediately.

FISH

Herrings and mackerel are very much part of the traditional diet in Wales, with the most common method of preparing them – soused in herbs and spices – still a favourite. A century ago it would have been a common sight in the autumn to see women with barrows selling fresh herrings in all the coastal towns, and even today after a very good catch every restaurant on the west coast will have herring on the menu.

Alas, the same can't be said for the other varieties of fish found off the Welsh coast. Hake, a favourite in the south, is rarely to be found on a Welsh fish stall, nor are local cod, haddock, plaice or whiting. Gone are the days when the fishing boats would bring their catch straight into Swansea harbour and the vans then took the fresh fish up the valleys for tea that day.

There has been a serious decline in investment in the Welsh fishing industry since the forties right up until the the last decade. Local fishing fleets dwindled and the once well-established rail routes from ports to markets were discontinued. Fish swam safely off the Welsh shore.

But now there is a revival. Holyhead has experienced a face-lift, and the docks at Milford Haven are seeing some investment too. Larger deep-sea trawlers are using the ports and the tonnage of fresh fish landed is increasing every year. But the large quay-side market is almost gone for ever and the dream of buying fish fresh off the boat is an illusion. Just about all the catch goes straight off to the enormous fish markets at Grimsby, Fleetwood or Billingsgate; across the Channel to France and Spain.

The good news is that fishing continues on a small scale from all the Welsh harbours. Local fishermen with their limited resources fish off the coasts, collecting whatever the season brings: herring and mackerel in the autumn; lobster, crab and scallops during the spring and summer; and a fairly general supply of flat fish that feed on the bottom of the sea bed. There is skate, halibut, plaice, lemon sole and brill, sometimes sea bass or grey mullet. Having no way of storing the fish on ice it can't be transported to the large fish markets; these are the fish that find their way into the small fish stalls, vans and local fish shops like Kim Fish in Penrhyn Bay, Bangor. Ask any restaurateur how he gets his fish and with a nod and a wink he'll say, 'First find your fisherman and then keep him a secret!'

Keith Rothwell at Ye Old Bull's Head in Beaumaris orders a stone of fresh flat or round fish and waits to see what arrives before he plans his menu. 'I don't mind what type of fish it is, as long as it's really fresh.'

It is wise to befriend a game fisherman, for silvery wild salmon run in many Welsh rivers: the Conway and Clwyd in the north, Mawddach and Rheidol on the west, Usk and Wye in the south and, perhaps most famous of all, the Teifi, Towyi and Cleddau in the south-western corner.

In fact, salmon were so prolific in the early part of this century that the Welsh became sick of eating it and written employment agreements for staff in rural areas dictated that salmon would be served no more than three times a week!

There is another fish, though, in these rivers that is cherished by the Welsh and that is their delicate sea trout, a strain of brown trout which they call *sewin*. It is similar to salmon in appearance but taste and texture differ slightly, being less oily. How to tell the difference? 'Just by looking at it,' the fishermen say; 'the mouth is different and the shape of the tail, but the sure sign is to count the rows of scales.'

Catching sewin is not easy whether you set out with a rod and line, in a coracle, which is a light circular boat, or using a net which you stretch across the mouth of a river. These fishing methods are granted only with a hefty licence, and there is a fair amount of acrimony between all the fishermen who are chasing that same fish! Anne Fitzgerald, at her Farmhouse Kitchen in Mathry in Dyfed, welcomes sewin throughout the season from April to August and fish appear on her kitchen table from a variety of fishermen.

As for coarse fishing, there are delicate grayling in the rivers and in the deep lakes of north Wales, such as Bala and Padarn, a fish left over from the ice age, the torgoch or red char. This must be one of the prettiest fish; speckled, with a rosy belly, it has a soft texture and a flavour so delicate you need add nothing but butter!

Brown river trout, enjoyed over the centuries by many rural families who had time to tickle and not money to buy, still tantalise the Welsh fisherman.

After all this talk of catching fish, let's get down to eating it and, more important, when to eat it. Is it better to leave fish overnight so that the flesh firms and the flavour may be more pronounced? The fishmonger may say so, but the professional cook, like Keith at Ye Old Bull's Head in Beaumaris, says he likes his fish *'just* dead'!

BRAISED FILLET OF SEWIN IN A DILL AND WHITE WINE SAUCE

The season for sewin, or Welsh sea trout, is March to August and they are found in many Welsh rivers. Sewin are the greatest prize for those men who fish with rod and line, although more sewin are caught by seine netsmen who lay their nets across the fast-flowing estuaries. On the Teifi coracles are still used to catch these fine fish. Similar to salmon in shape, but distinguishable by the shape of their mouths and the number of scales behind the dorsal fin, sewin also have a paler pink flesh and delicate flavour, with a softer texture due to a less oily content. For Anne Fitzgerald there is definitely no comparison between the two, and sewin wins hands down.

SERVES 4

2½ lb (1.25 kg) whole sewin
2 oz (50 g) or a big bunch of fresh dill
3½ fl oz (100 ml) Gewurztraminer wine

For the sauce:
3½ fl oz (100 ml) Gewurztraminer wine
3½ fl oz (100 ml) thick cream

2 egg yolks
chopped dill

keta (salmon eggs) or lumpfish roe or a snippet of dill to garnish

1   Pre-heat the oven to gas mark 7, 425°F (220°C).

2   Remove the two fillets from the sewin by cutting down each side of the backbone and easing the flesh from the bones. Skin the two long fillets and cut each in half.

3   Line the bottom of a casserole (cast-iron if possible) with fronds of fresh dill and pour over the wine. Place the fillets on the dill, spacing them as much as possible, then put the casserole on a medium flame until the wine bubbles.

4   Cover with a lid, leaving a slight gap for steam to escape, and put the casserole into the centre of the oven for 7–8 minutes. (When cooked the sewin fillets should be a fine pink colour and have small beads of moisture on the surface which shows they are not overcooked. Cooking time is extremely variable depending on the particular oven and the size of the fillets, so reliance on the eye rather than the clock is essential.)

5   Begin the sauce by heating the wine and cream together until almost boiling. Whisk, then pour into a bowl containing the 2 egg yolks and stir hard.

6   Strain this mixture back into the saucepan and heat gently (on no account let the sauce boil or it will curdle), whisking from time to time, until a smooth, quite thick sauce has formed. Add some chipped dill and keep warm over a very low heat.

7   Put the fillets on to four warm plates. Whisk the sauce one last time and pour it around the fish. Put some keta on the top of each fillet for garnish.

BASIC FISH STOCK

It's quick and easy to make fish stock: all you need is a handful of fish bones, a couple of vegetables and 20 minutes on the stove. So next time you go to a fishmonger ask for some fish trimmings and make up a large pot of stock. Simply divide it between empty yoghurt pots and store it away in the freezer. No matter what they say on the packets, the fish stock you can buy never tastes as good as the real thing. Surely your fish dishes deserve the best!

SERVES 4

1 lb (450 g) fish trimmings (bones, heads and tails, skin, shells)
1 stick celery
1 medium onion, peeled and diced
1 medium leek, chopped
a few parsley stalks
1 glass white wine
cold water

1   Put the trimmings and vegetables in a large saucepan, cover with cold water and bring to the boil. Turn down the heat and simmer gently for 20 minutes (no longer, or the stock will taste bitter).

2   Strain the liquid through a fine sieve or cloth and freeze.

FILLETS OF FISH BAKED IN A HERB CRUST

Fresh fish varies in price enormously according to the time of year and the weather, so ask your fishmonger for the best buy of the week. Mackerel is always cheap in the summer, especially if you can buy it in the harbour straight off the boat. This herb crust makes a healthy alternative to batter and almost any fish can be prepared in this way. Just toss the fillets in a mixture of fresh herbs and oatmeal and bake in the oven. Serve with a tangy yoghurt sauce and a salad.

SERVES 4

4 whole individual mackerel (gutted or filleted) or 1½–2 lb (750 g–1 kg) fresh fillets of mackerel (or cod, haddock, hake, plaice, sole or herring)

4 oz (100 g) plain flour, seasoned with salt and freshly ground black pepper

2 eggs

4 oz (100 g) stale brown breadcrumbs or medium oatmeal

1 tablespoon chopped fresh mixed herbs (parsley, dill, chervil etc)

1 teaspoon ground coriander seed

¼ teaspoon cayenne pepper (optional)

light cooking oil, e.g. sunflower, rapeseed or groundnut

Yoghurt sauce:

¼ pint (150 ml) plain yoghurt mixed with 1 teaspoon runny honey and the grated rind of half an orange

1   Pre-heat the oven to gas mark 4, 350°F (180°C)

2   Run the back of a knife over the surface of the fish fillets to check that there are no hidden bones in the flesh and remove all visible bones. Cut into portions.

3   Toss the fish in the seasoned flour. Whisk the egg and brush this over the floured fillets.

4   Combine the breadcrumbs or oatmeal with the herbs, coriander and cayenne. Pat this mixture on to the egged fish and press with a palette knife.

5   With kitchen paper, rub some oil over a baking tin. Dribble a little oil over the fish fillets and bake in the oven for 15 minutes or until the herb coating is crisp and golden.

6   Serve with the yoghurt sauce.

SKATE WITH WILD GARLIC BUTTER

Skate is now one of the cheapest fish to buy at often less than £1 per pound. Off the west coast of Wales, and particularly Milford Haven, it is brought in by the ton and cut up on the dockside. The wings are very meaty and don't have bones, just cartilage; they are easy to eat once you understand which way the cartilage lies. In this recipe the composition of the fish is visible since the wings are poached and served with a butter sauce.
Wild garlic, or ramsons, are found in profusion in damp woods and lanes throughout south Wales and they smell pleasantly garlicky when you walk through a bed of the pretty white-flowering plants in spring. Snipped into butter at the last minute, this herb adds just a hint of flavour, not as strong as the garlic bulb, but enough to cut into the richness of the sauce.

SERVES 4

1½ lb (675 g) skate
juice of ½ lemon
1 small onion
1 bay leaf
2–3 peppercorns
3–4 parsley stalks
½ teaspoon salt

Garlic butter:
3 oz (75 g) unsalted butter
juice of ½ lemon
1 level tablespoon chopped wild garlic
  leaves or 1 clove garlic, crushed to a
  paste with a little salt

1   Cut the skate into manageable pieces, and put them into a large saucepan, cover with water and add the lemon juice, onion, bay leaf, peppercorns, parsley stalks and salt.

2   Bring to the boil, and simmer very gently for 10 to 15 minutes, until the flesh turns opaque.

3   Carefully lift the cooked skate out of the pan and transfer to a warm serving dish.

4   Put the unsalted butter in the frying-pan and heat it over a fast flame until it foams and begins to turn brown. Add the squeezed lemon juice at once, toss in the chopped garlic leaves and pour over the skate.

5   Serve immediately, with freshly boiled noodles to soak up the butter sauce.

STEAMED FILLETS OF SEA BASS WITH ORANGE AND BASIL BUTTER SAUCE

As with any cook worth his salt, Keith Rothwell is pedantic about the preparation of his recipes. He acknowledges that sea bass is expensive and suggests that you buy one that is between 1½ and 3 pounds (750 g–1 kg). If a fish is under 1½ pounds or 14 inches (36 cm) long, it has been caught illegally below the limits set to preserve sea bass stocks, and if it is over 3 pounds the meat to bone ratio changes and the meat becomes more expensive. He also suggests that a cheaper fish could be steamed in the same way and served with his sauce. You may have a friendly fishmonger who will happily prepare your fish for you; if not, then follow Keith's careful instructions and you can't go wrong:

With a pair of sharp scissors, remove all the fins. Be very careful doing this as there are some very sharp spines running down the back and one on the underside. (If you do prick yourself, dress it with antiseptic straight away as this type of injury has a tendency to become easily inflamed.) Do not remove the fish's tail yet.
Hold on to the tail with a cloth and, using a fairly blunt knife, scrape away the scales. To avoid a mess this job can be done under water or with the fish suspended in a large plastic bin-sack.
Make an incision from the vent to the head and remove the guts. Wash in running water until thoroughly clean. Pat dry, then remove the tail with scissors.
Using a sharp knife, remove the fillets from the fish, one from each side of the body. Using a pair of pliers, remove all the bones that remain in or on the fillet. Divide the fillets into portions, allowing two pieces per person.

Keith cooked his sea bass in a domestic steamer, but a wire sieve suspended over a saucepan with a lid will work well.

SERVES 4

1 sea bass weighing 2½–3 lb (1.25–1.5 kg)	6 oz (175 g) butter
½ pint (300 ml) fish stock reduced to 2 fl oz (50 ml) – see page 29	freshly ground black pepper
juice of 1 orange	10 leaves fresh basil, shredded
2 fl oz (50 ml) cream	1 orange, peeled and cut into segments
	4 sprigs of basil

1 Bring 2 inches (5 cm) water to boil in the steamer base or saucepan. Arrange the fish fillets in the top of the steamer, or sieve, cover with a lid and simmer for about 5 minutes.

2 Combine the fish stock and orange juice in a small saucepan and bring to the boil. Keep the mixture boiling until it has reduced to about 2 tablespoons and is thick and syrupy.

3 Add the cream and return to the boil for a minute, stirring all the time. Turn the heat right down low and add the butter to the sauce, little by little, whisking all the time so that it emulsifies into the stock.

4 When all the butter has been added and the sauce is creamy, add pepper to taste and the shredded basil and leave the sauce, covered, in a warm place.

5 Transfer the sea bass straight on to warm serving plates, two pieces each; one piece skin side down, the other skin side up, and pour the sauce over.

6 Garnish with orange segments and sprigs of basil.

SEA BASS MARINADED WITH FRESH HERBS

Keith Rothwell from Ye Old Bull's Head in Beaumaris on Anglesey certainly knows his fish – but he's not sure that the rest of us do. This is the advice he gives when shopping for fish.
'The fish must be super-fresh! Choose a fish that has bright red gills, eyes that are slightly protruding and shiny, and skin which is wet and shiny and not dried – as this makes the process of scaling almost impossible. The flesh should be firm and springy, and it must not have a fishy smell, it should smell only of fresh seawater.'
If sea bass is outside your budget Keith suggests using another cheaper firm-fleshed fish such as monkfish or turbot.

SERVES 4

12 oz (350 g) fillet of sea bass

Marinade:
¼ pint (150 ml) extra virgin olive oil (or the best you can find)
1 fl oz (25 ml) fresh lime juice

a handful of fresh herbs (tarragon, chervil, dill, parsley, chives, fennel, thyme etc) – use less of the stronger ones. Leave them as a whole leaf; don't chop.
1 teaspoon salt

1   Place the fillet, skin side down, on a flat surface. Using a narrow-bladed, razor-sharp knife and starting from the middle of the fillet going towards the tail, slice the flesh as thinly as you possibly can – thin enough to read a newspaper through if possible.

2   Lay some slices on a sheet of clingfilm or greaseproof paper; pour over a little of the marinade; then another sheet of paper; then a layer of fish, and so on.

3   Leave for at least 12 hours, or up to three days in a fridge.

4   Serve at room temperature, arranged over a large flat plate, just as it is.

TROUT WRAPPED IN BACON

This recipe is traditional rural Wales: local trout – possibly poached – sitting in a dish wrapped in fat bacon from last year's family pig. The tastes mix perfectly together, with the richness from the bacon complementing the clean mildness of the fish. I like to pop some fresh chopped chives in the empty belly of the fish together with a good slice of lemon. I find smoked streaky bacon works the best.
For those who hate bones, why not take them out of the trout before you start? This is what you do:

First gut the fish and clean under cold running water. Cut off the head, tail and fins. Open out the split fish and spread it flat, skin side up. Press firmly along the centre back of the fish to loosen the backbone, then turn the fish over. Starting at the head end, ease away the backbone with the tip of a knife, removing at the same time as many of the small bones as possible.

Your trout is now spineless and ready to cook!

SERVES 4

4 good-sized trout, brown if possible, otherwise rainbow
1 tablespoon chopped chives
4 slices of lemon
salt and freshly ground black pepper
8 rashers smoked streaky bacon

Sauce:
Greek yoghurt mixed with a little fresh grated horseradish and chopped parsley

1   Pre-heat the oven to gas mark 4, 350°F (180°C).

2   Clean, gut, and possibly bone, the trout. Put some chopped chives and a slice of lemon in the belly of each fish and season with salt and pepper.

3   Wrap each fish in two rashers of bacon and lay them side by side in a baking dish.

4   Bake for 15–20 minutes until the bacon is crisp on top and the trout flesh cooked and flaky.

5   Serve with the horseradish sauce.

FILLETS OF PLAICE WITH A HERB MOUSSE

This recipe makes a spectacular light lunch or supper dish for four; the filled and rolled fillets of plaice are served on a bed of spinach with some tangy hollandaise sauce over the top.
Fillets of plaice are available frozen but if you can shop at a traditional fishmonger fresh plaice usually has a better flavour and always a firmer texture, which is helpful when rolling the fillets. A pinch of salt on your fingers will help you grip the tail while skinning the plaice – alternatively ask the fishmonger to skin it for you.

SERVES 4

8 fillets of plaice
8 oz (225 g) garlic-flavoured cream cheese
1 oz (25 g) chopped parsley
1 egg yolk
salt and black pepper
4 oz (100 g) prawns, cooked and peeled
juice of 1 lemon
1 lb (450 g) fresh spinach

Herb hollandaise sauce:
3 tablespoons white wine vinegar
1 tablespoon water
6 black peppercorns
1 bayleaf
3 egg yolks
6 oz (175 g) soft unsalted butter
1 tablespoon chopped fresh mixed herbs
salt and black pepper

1   Skin the fillets, wash and pat them dry.

2   Blend the cream cheese with the parsley and egg yolk until smooth, adding salt and pepper to taste. Stir in the prawns.

3   Sprinkle each fillet with salt and pepper and a little lemon juice; lay 2 teaspons of the stuffing on each and roll up.

4   Place the rolled fillets side by side in a colander, sieve or top part of a steamer and steam over a pan of fast-boiling water for 8 minutes. Alternatively cook in the microwave following your model instructions.

5   Clean and cook the spinach; drain and mash to a pulp. Keep warm in a heat-proof serving dish.

6   In a small saucepan boil the vinegar and water with the peppercorns and bayleaf until reduced to 1 tablespoon. Leave to cool.

7   In a small bowl cream the egg yolks with a walnut-sized piece of butter and a pinch of salt. Strain the vinegar into the eggs, and set the bowl over a pan of boiling water. Turn off the heat.

8 Whisk in the remaining butter, little by little, until the sauce is shiny and has the consistency of thick cream. Stir in the herbs and season to taste with salt and pepper.

9 Heat your grill to its hottest. Put the cooked fillets on top of the spinach and spoon over the hollandaise sauce. Flash under the grill until brown. Serve at once with some crisp French bread.

ARCTIC CHAR BAKED IN FOIL

I've shared a few fish with my friend John Ellis Roberts, the chief warden of the Snowdonia National Park, but none I have enjoyed more than the Arctic Char or Torgoch that we ate together on the banks of Lake Padarn. 'Torgoch is the Welsh name for Char and it means literally red belly,' John told me. I was thrilled to see this rare and beautiful fish, with pink spots on a shimmering brown skin with a pretty pink belly, its mouth is like that of a salmon. The flesh is pink, firm and well flavoured without being at all muddy.

It's hard to catch because the char lives deep under the surface of the lake, so fishermen use a heavier weight on their line. They prefer to use oars rather than an engine on the small fishing boats because speed causes the line to rise.

In the late summer though the fish surface and head for the river to spawn. Since they are nearer the surface a spinner will catch them. I suggest that Char taste best eaten as fresh as possible, but please don't go lighting fires beside any lake without first having asked permission.

This is how I like to eat my Char:
Gut and cook the Torgoch whole – simply wrapped in buttered foil with some fresh herbs and a sprinkle of salt and pepper.
If you cook over an open fire or barbecue, let the embers die right down and lay the tinfoil-wrapped fish straight onto the cooling ashes. Turn over once, and let the fish cook for about 10 minutes in all.
In the oven, cook the Char in a similar fashion for about 10–15 minutes at gas mark 4, 350°F (180°C).

SERVES 4

SUPPER HERRINGS WITH SAGE AND APPLES

The seasonal earnings from selling herrings, a job often taken up by women, were useful before Christmas. During the autumn glut plump fresh herrings were on everyone's menu. Many a schoolchild used to take his herring, fresh, soused or smoked, to school for a snack during the winter.
This is a typical family recipe, similar to one I have eaten in Scandinavia. The combination of the fish with apples and sage is very pleasant and delightfully inexpensive.

SERVES 4

4 herrings	1 large onion, peeled and sliced
English mustard	1 teaspoon sage, chopped (fresh if
salt and pepper	possible)
1 lb (450 g) potatoes, peeled and sliced	1 oz (25 g) butter
2 cooking apples, peeled and sliced	10 fl oz (300 ml) dry cider

1 Pre-heat the oven to gas mark 4, 350°F (180°C).

2 Butter a 3 pint (1.75 litre) baking dish.

3 Clean and fillet the herrings. (See Trout Wrapped in Bacon, p. 35, for filleting technique.) Spread the fillets with a thin layer of mustard, salt and pepper and roll up.

4 Line the bottom of the dish, using half the potatoes, and arrange the rolled herring fillets on top. Scatter over the apple slices and then the sliced onions, and sprinkle over the sage.

5 Arrange the remaining potatoes on the top. Dot with butter and pour the cider around the side of the dish. Cover and bake for 1 hour.

6 Turn the heat up to gas mark 7, 425°F (220°C) for another 15 minutes to brown the top.

7 Serve this filling fish dish with nothing more than a glass of cider!

CRAB PASTA

Pasta came to Wales some time ago with the large immigrant Italian population who arrived during the boom years of the steel and coal industries. The Italians opened cafés in the south Wales valleys, moving into all sections of catering as time went on. So Wales is fortunate to have the best of Italian ingredients imported regularly by a community who really understands about al dente pasta.
I usually prepare this crab sauce in a large bowl in my microwave oven while the pasta is boiling on the conventional cooker. Once it is drained, I simply stir the pasta into the sauce and bingo, we're ready to dine!

SERVES 4

1 tablespoon cooking oil
1 teaspoon salt
6 rashers streaky bacon, cut into strips
1 onion, finely chopped
2 cloves garlic, crushed with salt
8 oz (225 g) cooked fresh crab (or tinned)
1 tablespoon chopped parsley

3½ fl oz (100 ml) dry white wine
salt
½ teaspoon cayenne pepper
½ pint (300 ml) double cream
8–10 oz (225–275 g) pasta twirls or shells
freshly grated parmesan

1 Put a large saucepan of water on to boil; add the cooking oil and salt.

2 In a medium-sized saucepan or heavy-based casserole dish, dry-fry the bacon strips gently without any added fat on top of the cooker. Once the bacon fat begins to run, add the onion and garlic and cook briskly until the onion is almost soft but not brown.

3 Toss in the crab, parsley, white wine and seasoning, bring to the boil and stir in the cream. Heat through.

4 Cook the pasta in the boiling water, drain through a colander and rinse with hot water to prevent it sticking together; arrange in a large serving bowl.

5 Pour over the crab sauce and hand round the parmesan cheese separately.

SALMON AND MONKFISH KEBAB WITH WATERCRESS MAYONNAISE AND SAFFRON RICE

Fashion does funny things with food. Salmon, once a luxury, is now overproduced in fish farms, and monkfish, always considered an ugly and unworthy fish, is now prized for its taste and texture. In fact, the monkfish may cost more than the salmon. The rich oiliness of the salmon is ideal for kebabs since it loses little of its moisture under the direct heat of the grill. I like to serve a watercress mayonnaise with the kebabs, but for a healthier sauce use fromage frais or yoghurt instead.

SERVES 4

12 oz (350 g) fresh salmon tail end or
   cutlets
12 oz (350 g) monkfish tail
3 tablespoons olive oil
2 tablespoons lemon juice
1 tablespoon chopped chives
salt and pepper
1 lemon, quartered

For the watercress mayonnaise:
8 tablespoons mayonnaise
4 tablespoons finely chopped watercress

For the saffron rice:
1 packet saffron strands or ¼ teaspoon
   saffron powder
1 oz (25 g) butter
1 small onion, finely chopped
8 oz (225 g) long grain rice
¾ pint (450 ml) hot fish or chicken stock
salt and freshly ground black pepper

1   Skin and bone the fish, cut in neat cubes and put them in a bowl. Pour over the olive oil and lemon juice, and stir in the chopped chives. Leave for 3 to 4 hours, then thread the cubes on to 4 skewers.

2   Grill slowly, turning often, basting with the oil and lemon juice.

3   Serve with lemon quarters and watercress mayonnaise on a bed of saffron rice.

4   Pre-heat the oven to gas mark 4, 350°F (180°C).

5   Soak the saffron in 3 tablespoons hot water for 10 minutes.

6   In a heavy-based casserole melt the butter and fry the onion gently for 5 minutes. Toss in the rice and fry, stirring continuously until the rice looks transparent.

7   Pour in the stock, season and add the saffron water.

8   Cover the casserole and bake in the oven for 15–18 minutes, until the rice is cooked and all the stock absorbed. (Add a little boiling water if the rice gets too dry.)

MACKEREL BAKED WITH FENNEL

'He who sees fennel and gathers it not, is not a man but a devil.' – a noteworthy quote from a Welsh physician of the past.
Bright-eyed, glistening green and blue, mackerel fresh from the sea taste great. With sophisticated ice-packing services at major Welsh ports now, fresh mackerel are transported nationwide.
Rich in polyunsaturated fats, and particularly high in the omega three series (esential oils which are believed to lower the risk of heart disease), mackerel is one of the healthiest foods to eat. Fennel, I find, cuts the oily rich flavour.
I suggest serving crisp salty samphire with the mackerel. This seaweed grows on the sandflats around the Pembrokeshire coast and on the Menai Straits; fishmongers usually stock it during the summer and will, I am sure, find you some if you ask. Here is a recipe that takes very little time to prepare and is full of flavour.

SERVES 4

fresh samphire
4 medium-sized mackerel, gutted
1 tablespoon French mustard
juice of 1 lemon

salt and freshly ground black pepper
a really good bunch of fresh fennel
olive oil

1   Pre-heat the oven to gas mark 9, 475°F (240°C).

2   Pick over the samphire and blanch it by putting it into cold water and bringing to the boil. Drain and rinse immediately.

3   Wash the mackerel and spread a quarter of the mustard inside each one. Sprinkle in the lemon juice, salt, lots of pepper, and a good sprig of fennel. Brush the outside with olive oil.

4   Wrap each fish in foil and bake in a hot oven for 10–12 minutes.

5   Serve out of the foil with their juices poured over them, sitting on a bed of samphire.

CHEESE AND VEGETABLE DISHES

Viva vegetarianism!

No longer thought of as cranks. Their choice of diet is something that more and more of us are turning to.

However, not so long ago in Wales, times were so hard that a large part of the population had little choice but to live off dairy products, grains, fish and the vegetables that they grew themselves.

This point is illustrated by Mrs Minwell Tibbott, who is Assistant Keeper in the Department of Buildings and Domestic Life at the Welsh Folk Museum, St Fagans, South Glamorgan. In her book *Welsh Fare* she records a huge collection of recipes for oat-based gruel-type dishes that were part of everyday life at the turn of the century.

Meatless Glamorgan sausages, made from leeks, cheese and bread-crumbs, are a fine example of frugality made tasty, and of course Welsh rarebit is almost a national dish.

The Welsh are natural scavengers of wild food; living off the land, they know how good fresh fruit and vegetables really taste, especially when they are free! Visit vegetarian Elunid Lloyd at the Cnapan Guesthouse in Newport, Pembrokeshire, and you can be sure of a fine 'green' welcome. Time permitting, Elunid will have spent the afternoon down by the shore gathering natural specialities such as samphire, laver seaweed, young nettles, sea spinach and wild fennel to include in her vegetarian dish of the day. She always has a range of local cheeses on the cheeseboard, most of which find their way into her cooking too.

Organic farming may be a new concept in many parts of Britain, but in Wales some farms have never been anything else!

Rachael and Gareth Rowlands at Brynlys Farm near Aberystwyth run the perfect example of natural mixed farming where crop rotation and a variety of livestock allow them to produce a wide range of organic products. Just taste their butter made from the milk of Guernsey cows which have lived on a natural diet of grass and clover. Wonderful! And try a basket of farm-grown vegetables – but leave the tops for the farm pigs, who naturally live off swill rather than premixed feedstuff.

If the Rowlandses can make a living out of natural farming, one wonders why we, the consumers, should accept anything else? Certainly with some of the meat processing that is apparent today, it is no wonder that the swing towards organic foods grows apace.

Cheese is produced organically too in Wales and there is a depth and individualism to Welsh cheese that is hard to beat. Bad press over the past few years has done the farmhouse cheese producers no good, but a health scare certainly brings hygiene to the fore and we, the consumers, can only benefit. If pasteurisation, when the milk must be heated to 63°C for 30 minutes thus killing all good as well as bad bacteria, becomes a compulsory process, though, one wonders if the character of individual cheeses won't be lost.

Cheese-making was, at one time, an integral part of farm life in Wales, but during the war years limited milk supplies allowed the skills to be forgotten and it is only over the last 20 years that cheese has been made again commercially. Then with the arrival of milk quotas many dairy farmers turned their surplus milk into cheese and now we enjoy farmhouse goat's, ewe's and cow's milk cheese.

As with any new industry set up in a rural area, distribution becomes a major problem and we, the buying public, suffer from not being able to get many of the Welsh farmhouse cheeses. There are a couple of enterprising delivery services who collect from the farms and take the cheeses to the shops, hotels and restaurants. Almost everywhere you go, it is now possible to find a Welsh cheeseboard in Wales. So look for Welsh cheeses, and these are a few names to spot.

ACORN, made in Bethania, near Llanon in Dyfed. A ewe's milk cheese, full fat, hard pressed, with vegetarian rennet. The majority of the milk is home produced and completely free from herbicides, pesticides and chemical fertilisers. Acorn may be a suitable substitute for those allergic to cow's or goat's milk.

*

CARDIGAN, made in Lampeter from organic cow's milk with vegetarian rennet. In texture a cross between a Cheddar and Caerphilly, mild in flavour when young but matures well. Available all the year round in discs of 7½– 8 lb (3.25–3.5 kg).

*

CASTLE HYWEL, made in Narberth, Dyfed, Cheddar, Caerphilly. A soft cheese with nuts and other ingredients.

43

CAWS CENARTH, traditional Caerphilly and Cheddar made from the farm herd of pedigree Friesian and Holstein dairy cattle. The cheeses are sold in presentation boxes of 14 oz (400 g) or 2 lb (1 kg) and 9 lb (4 kg) wheels.

*

CAWS CARON, made in Tregaron, Dyfed. A hard pressed goat's cheese made by the same method as Caerphilly. Smoked Caws Caron is also available.

*

LLANBOIDY, made in Login, Whitland, Dyfed. An old-style, hard, full fat cheese from milk of the rare Red Poll cattle. Available in natural mature flavour or with laver seaweed.

*

LLANGLOFFAN, made in Castle Morris, Dyfed. A hard, full fat, naturally rinded cheese made from unpasteurised milk from a Jersey herd of cows. Also available with chives and garlic.

*

MAESLLYN, made in Llandyssul, Dyfed. One of the first Caerphilly cheeses to be produced in recent years. A traditional farmhouse Caerphilly, brined and matured for 6–8 weeks. Smoked Caerphilly is also available. Jill Bond also makes a mature Cheddar as well as CAETHWAS soft cheese mixed with herbs, garlic and wine.

*

MAES MAWR, made in Llanllyfni, Caernarfon. A hard pressed goat's cheese with natural crust.

*

MERLIN, made in Ystrad Meurig, Dyfed. A hard goat's cheese, plain or flavoured with olives.

*

NEVERN DAIRIES CHEESE, made in Nevern, Dyfed. Traditional Cheddar.

*

PANTLLYN, made in Carmarthen, Dyfed. Farmhouse Cheddar, also ABERNANT, made from part cow's, part goat's milk.

*

PANT-YS-GAWN, made in Mamhilad, Pontypool. A soft white creamy cheese made from pasteurised goat's milk using vegetarian rennet. Mild non-goaty flavour, easily spread. Available plain, with herbs, coated with black pepper, green and red sweet pepper, and citrus peel.

*

PENCARREG, made in Lampeter, Dyfed. A full fat soft cow's milk cheese, similar to Brie.

*

PEN Y BONT, made in Carmarthen, Dyfed. A hard goat's cheese.

*

PLAS DAIRY FARM CHEESE, made in Anglesey. Low fat, spreadable cow's and goat's cheese. Made from lactic curd in a variety of flavours such as lamb pastrami, smoked venison with garlic and black pepper, or smoked salmon and parsley.

*

SKIRRID EWE'S MILK CHEESE, made in Bethania with Acorn. Using unpasteurised sheep's milk, pure sea salt and vegetarian rennet, the cheeses are marinaded in Elizabethan mead before being taken to maturing for three months prior to being sold. A firm white cheese with a natural rind and mild flavour.

*

TEIFI CHEESE, made in Llandyssul, Dyfed. A Gouda-type cheese; semi-hard with a creamy texture. Low fat, made from unpasteurised milk, partly skimmed. Low-sodium salt used. Flavours: plain, chives, cumin seed, garlic, celery and garlic, garlic and onion, nettle, mustard seed or sweet pepper.

*

T'YN GRUG, made in Lampeter, Dyfed. Mature farmhouse Cheddar made with organically produced cow's milk.

*

WAUGRON, made in Whitland, Dyfed. A Colby-type cheese.

To my mind Welsh cheese is best eaten in Wales, bought from the farm where it is produced. Visitors are encouraged to watch the cheese being made and can learn something of the history of the cheese and the traditional methods of cheesemaking. I think this is an experience that no traveller to Wales should miss.

THREE-CHEESE SOUFFLÉ

The word soufflé means 'puffed up' in French, and that is exactly what a soufflé is.
The air whisked into the egg white expands as it heats and causes the soufflé to rise.
It is its lightness of texture and delicate flavour that make a soufflé so good to eat.
They are also extremely easy to make; just follow three basic rules and you won't fail.
1. Make a good thick panade, or white sauce, which will hold the whisked egg whites
and let them expand.
2. Whisk the egg whites to a firm snow and fold them evenly and thoroughly into the
panade.
3. Relax in the knowledge that your soufflé will be a huge success and don't peep into
the oven until the cooking time is up!
In this recipe I have combined three cheeses with different flavours and varying
textures. Adapt the recipe to the cheeses you find locally, but stick to these quantities.

SERVES 4

2 oz (50 g) butter
2 oz (50 g) plain white flour
½ pint (300 ml) milk
a few drops Tabasco sauce
3 eggs, separated
2 oz (50 g) Teifi or Gouda-type cheese, grated

2 oz (50 g) low-fat soft cow's milk cheese (Plas Farm or soft fresh Welsh goat's cheese)
a handful of chives, chopped
1 oz (25 g) smoked Tudor ewe's milk cheese (or any smoked farmhouse cheese, grated)

1 Pre-heat the oven to gas mark 6, 400°F (200°C).

2 Butter a 7 inch (18 cm) 2 pint (1 litre) soufflé dish. Melt the butter over a medium heat and stir in the flour. Cook until bubbles appear, then pour in the milk. Bring back to the boil, whisking all the time until the mixture is well blended and smooth. Add the Tabasco sauce and leave the sauce to cool a little.

3 Stir in the egg yolks and the Teifi cheese.

4 Whisk the egg whites until firm (so that they don't fall out of the bowl if you turn it upside down). Using a spatula or large metal spoon, fold them into the soufflé, making sure that there are no lumps.

5 Spoon half the soufflé mixture into the prepared dish. Sprinkle over the cow's or goat's cheese in a layer, cover with the chives and pour in the remaining soufflé mixture.

6 Sprinkle the smoked Tudor cheese over the top of the soufflé and place the dish on a baking sheet.

7 Bake in the oven for 20–25 minutes or until the soufflé has risen and is golden brown and the middle wobbles a little when pushed.

8 Serve the soufflé at once with chunks of crisp fresh bread and a salad made from tomatoes, fresh basil and olive oil.

WELSH RAREBIT

It seems that the Welsh have loved their toasted cheese since medieval times. But until the Victorian era toasted cheese was just that: a slice of ewe's or cow's milk cheese was simply toasted in front of the fire and served on a slice of bread or toast. The combination of ale and cheese in a sauce to be spread over toast is a more recent innovation, most probably borrowed from over the border where the English produced good hard farmhouse Cheddar to give the rarebit the sharpness it needs. Ale is usually served with Welsh Rarebit.

SERVES 4

8 oz (225 g) mature Welsh farmhouse Cheddar like T'yn Grug, Llangloffan or Llanboidy
1 oz (25 g) butter
1 tablespoon Worcestershire sauce

1 tablespoon English mustard
1 tablespoon flour
approximately 4 tablespoons beer
4 slices wholemeal bread
cayenne pepper

1 Grate the cheddar and mix it gradually with the remaining ingredients until you have a firm paste.

2 Toast the bread, then spread the cheese paste evenly over one side of each slice.

3 Grill gently until the topping is cooked through and well browned.

4 Dust the cooked rarebit with cayenne pepper and serve hot.

GLAMORGAN SAUSAGES WITH PLUM CHUTNEY

I dare say it was the economics of producing a sausage without any meat in it that made Glamorgan sausages so popular with the Welsh. Containing cheese, breadcrumbs, leeks and herbs, these tasty sausages were mentioned by George Borrow in his book, Wild Wales, *written in 1862. Alas, the cheese Glamorgan, from which they got their name, is no longer made, but Caerphilly is thought to be a direct descendant and gives these sausages a good texture and flavour.*

SERVES 4

5 oz (150 g) fresh breadcrumbs
1 small leek, finely chopped
3 oz (75 g) Caerphilly cheese, grated
1 tablespoon fresh parsley, chopped
salt and pepper
pinch of dry mustard
3 eggs
flour
oil or bacon fat for frying
extra breadcrumbs for coating

For the chutney:
2 lb (1 kg) plums, stoned
4 oz (100 g) dried fruit
1 tablespoon pickling spice
1 teaspoon salt
1 teaspoon ground ginger
1 teaspoon chilli powder
½ pint (300 ml) vinegar
12 oz (350 g) demerara sugar

1   Mix together the breadcrumbs, leek, cheese, parsley, seasonings and mustard.

2   Beat together 2 eggs and 1 yolk and use this to bind the mixture, adding a little milk if the mixture is still too dry to hold together.

3   Divide into 12, roll into sausage shapes and toss in flour.

4   Beat the remaining egg white until frothy; brush over the sausages, then coat them in the extra breadcrumbs. Chill in the fridge for 20 minutes.

5   Fry gently in oil or bacon fat until crisp and golden brown on all sides.

The chutney:

6   Simmer the plums and dried fruit, pickling spice (tied securely in muslin bag – I use the toe from a clean pair of tights or stocking), salt, ground ginger and chilli powder in a saucepan with just enough vinegar to stop the mixture from burning. Cook gently until the fruit is soft, stirring from time to time.

7   Add the remaining vinegar and stir in the sugar thoroughly.

8   Boil the chutney steadily until the mixture is thick. Remove the spice bag.

9   Pour the chutney into hot clean jars and seal.

GREEN RICE

An Italian might disagree, but I think that nothing cooks a risotto better than a microwave. The penetrating heat of the microwaves cooks the rice to a soft creamy texture without the grains breaking up, and the flavour is superb. Rather than Parmesan cheese, serve a bowl of freshly grated farmhouse Cheddar such as Llangloffan, made by Leon Downey in Castle Morris, Dyfed, from the milk of Jersey cows.

SERVES 4

3 pints (1.75 litres) chicken stock
1 tablespoon olive oil
3 medium-sized leeks, washed and
   chopped
10 oz (275 g) Italian short-grain rice

1 lb (450 g) fresh spinach, cooked
   (or 8 oz (225 g) frozen)
2 cloves garlic, crushed with salt
salt and freshly ground black pepper
freshly grated Llangloffan farmhouse
   Cheddar

Either use a large, heavy-based casserole and cook the risotto on top of the stove or prepare in the microwave using the appropriate dish.

1   Heat the chicken stock.

2   Heat the oil and cook the leeks until soft; add the rice and cook until it looks transparent, about 3 minutes. Add the spinach and garlic, stir well and pour on two-thirds of the chicken stock, plus seasoning.

3   Cover and simmer the risotto on a low heat for about 20 minutes. Check from time to time and add the remaining stock if the rice begins to look dry. The finished risotto should be creamy and green!

4   Serve with the grated cheese.

LAYERED HERB PANCAKE

The Welsh have a passion for pancakes and this recipe is fast becoming a Celtic classic! These herb-speckled pancakes look pretty when piled high on the plate. The filling is spread between the flat pancakes which are layered into a stack and the whole is cut like a cake.
I particularly like the variety of textures in this unusual dish.

SERVES 4

10 fl oz (300 ml) skimmed milk
1 egg
1 tablespoon chopped fresh mixed herbs
1 tablespoon melted butter
2 oz (50 g) plain wholemeal flour
2 oz (50 g) plain white flour
8 oz (225 g) Caerphilly cheese, crumbled

¼ pint (150 ml) double cream
cayenne or chilli pepper
salt
1 large or 2 medium leeks, finely chopped
1 oz (25 g) butter
6 oz (175 g) flat field mushrooms, sliced

1 Prepare the batter in a liquidiser by first pouring in the milk, then the egg, herbs and butter and finally the flour. Whizz until you have a smooth batter. Leave to thicken for 30 minutes.

2 For the first filling, mix 6 oz (175 g) of the cheese with the cream and season well with the cayenne pepper and a little salt.

3 For the second filling, fry the leeks in the butter for 4 minutes, then add the mushrooms and cook for another 3 minutes. Season well.

4 Heat a middle-sized frying-pan and fry the pancakes, maintaining a medium heat. Oil the pan for only the first one, thereafter dry-frying them as thinly as possible. You should make about 12. (Don't worry if the first pancake tears; it can sit unnoticed at the bottom of the dish, and by the time you get to the top of the pile, your pancakes will no doubt be perfect).

5 Butter a heatproof dish and lay a pancake flat on the bottom. Then, alternating the fillings, pile up the pancakes flat on top of each other. The result should look like a pancake dome.

6 Sprinkle the remaining cheese and a knob of butter on top and bake in a hot oven for 15 minutes, or grill gently for 10 minutes.

CREAMY BAKED CABBAGE

This recipe from Yves Monin is just right for those of us who hate cabbage. Yves, who used to run the charming Bakestone Restaurant in Caernarfon, has a way with cabbage, taking away any harshness and giving it a subtle creamy flavour. He first cooks the cabbage in a mixture of milk and water, then finishes it off with cream, nutmeg and a nutty-flavoured cheese such as Teifi or Gruyère.
This dish can be prepared and half-cooked early, then finished off with cream and baked when you want to serve it.

SERVES 4

2–3 lb (1–1.25 kg) savoy cabbage
½–1 pint (300–600 ml) milk and water
   mixed
¼ pint (150 ml) double cream

salt and freshly ground black pepper
nutmeg, grated
4 oz (100 g) Teifi (Gouda type) or
   Gruyère, grated

1   Pre-heat the oven to gas mark 7, 425°F (220°C).

2   Peel away the outer leaves from the cabbage; cut it in half and remove the inner core, then chop the remainder coarsely. Put it in a saucepan or microwave dish, cover with the mixture of milk and water, and cook until the cabbage is cooked but still crisp.

3   Drain well and arrange in a heatproof casserole dish. Pour over the cream, season well with salt, pepper and nutmeg and stir to mix.

4   Sprinkle over the cheese and bake in a hot oven for 10 minutes until the top is a rich golden brown.

PASTAI PEN Y BONT

It is nothing to eat a salad containing at least 10 wild ingredients at Cnapan Hotel in Newport, Pembrokeshire. 'Oh, they grow in the garden,' or 'I found them down in the estuary,' says Elunid Lloyd as you ask how she can serve wild fennel, samphire, nettle tops and sea spinach at one meal.
Her love of natural local ingredients brings constant surprise and change to the vegetarian menu which flourishes at Cnapan.
Elunid bakes this pasta in a heatproof dish measuring 10 inches (25 cm) in diameter and 3 inches (7.5 cm) deep.

SERVES 4

For the sauce:
3 tablespoons olive or sunflower oil
1 medium onion, chopped
1 clove garlic, crushed
1 teaspoon fresh grated root ginger
2 heaped tablespoons flour
1 pint (600 ml) milk
2 tablespoons stem ginger, chopped
salt and freshly ground black pepper
1 tablespoon Greek yoghurt

For the wheat layer:
2 tablespoons olive oil
4 oz (100 g) bulgar wheat, soaked in
   boiling water for 10 minutes
¼ teaspoon grated nutmeg

2 tablespoons elixir raisins
1 stick celery, finely chopped

For the spinach and nettle layer:
1 lb (450 g) fresh spinach or a mixture of
   spinach, young nettle tops, sorrel leaves
   and laverbread
1 tablespoon oil
1 oz (25 g) butter
1 orange, grated zest and juice
seasoning

Cheese layers:
4 oz (100 g) Pencarreg (Brie type), sliced
2 oz (50 g) Llanboidy (farmhouse
   Cheddar), grated

1 Pre-heat the oven to gas mark 5, 375°F (190°C).

2 Heat the oil in a saucepan and cook the onion gently until soft but not brown; add the garlic and ginger and cook for another minute, stirring all the time.

3 Stir in the flour, cook until it bubbles, then add the milk and bring the sauce to the boil, stirring as it thickens. Add the ginger, seasoning to taste, and the yoghurt.

4 To make the wheat layer, heat the oil in a saucepan, add the drained bulgar wheat and cover with a lid. Turn the heat off and leave the wheat to swell over gentle heat for 4–5 minutes, then add the nutmeg, raisins and celery.

5   To make the spinach and nettle layer, first snip or tear the greens, and soak in cold water for 5 minutes. In a large pan, heat the oil and melt the butter, toss in the wet greens and cook, covered, till they wilt (4–5 minutes). Continue cooking for a few minutes without the lid to evaporate all the juices. Add the orange zest and juice and seasoning to taste.

6   Spread half of the sauce over the bottom of a large ovenproof dish. Cover this with half of the bulgar wheat, then half of the spinach mixture.

7   Now add the Pencarreg slices right across the dish. Arrange the rest of the bulgar over the cheese, then spread the remaining spinach on top.

8   Cover the pie with the rest of the sauce and scatter the Llanboidy over the surface.

9   Bake for 30–40 minutes until bubbling and crispy brown on top.

Elunid sometimes sprinkles the top of the pastai with fresh breadcrumbs which have been lightly fried in butter. They give a lovely crunchy finish to this tasty dish.

SPINACH AND CAERPHILLY PASTY

The Welsh have a passion for pastry. Just visit a bakery and you will find the most surprising array of pastries and pasties: chicken and ham, beef and onion or cheese with anything!
My favourite pastry is rough puff, made with butter. It makes a nice crisp case for this family-sized pasty, keeping the filling of rice, eggs, Caerphilly cheese, spinach and herbs tightly pressed together.

SERVES 4

For the rough puff pastry:
8 oz (225 g) plain flour
6 oz (175 g) butter or firm margarine
¼ pint (150 ml) ice-cold water

For the filling:
6 oz (175 g) cooked rice, brown for
   preference
4 eggs, hard boiled, shelled and sliced
1 lb (450 g) fresh spinach, cooked and
   chopped
4 oz (100 g) Caerphilly cheese, crumbled

2 bunches spring onions, chopped
2 tablespoons chopped parsley
1 tablespoon ground coriander seeds
3 oz (75 g) butter, melted
salt and freshly ground black pepper
1 egg yolk

1   Pre-heat the oven to gas mark 7, 425°F (220°C).

2   Sift the flour with a pinch of salt into a mixing-bowl; cut the butter into walnut-sized pieces and mix with the flour using a palette knife. Pour in the water and mix quickly, then turn the dough on to a lightly floured board.

3   Roll the pastry out to an oblong, fold in three and give a half-turn to bring the open edges in front of you. Repeat the rolling and folding process twice, then chill the pastry for 20 minutes.

4   Roll the pastry out and fold it once more if it still looks streaky. It is now ready to use. Roll out the pastry to an oblong 10 × 12 inches (25 × 30 cm).

5   Arrange the filling down the centre: first the cooked rice, covered by the sliced eggs, chopped spinach, crumbled cheese, spring onions, herbs and spices. Finally pour over the melted butter and seasoning.

6   Make cuts in the outer 2 inches (5 cm) of the pastry so that it has a feathered effect; fold these strips from both sides across the filling so that you make a lattice, rather like a large plait. Whisk the egg yolk with a tablespoon of cold water and brush this over the pastry.

7   Bake in the oven for 20 minutes, then turn down the heat to gas mark 4, 350°F (180°C) for a further 10 minutes.

8   Serve the pasty warm with a salad and some sour cream, mixed with chopped chives.

CREAMED PARSNIPS

Root vegetables have always been a staple food in Wales. Used as a basis for cawl, the traditional Welsh soup, and often puréed and mixed together, swede, turnip and parsnip are favourites here.
The TV series production assistant, Valmai Williams, remembers her mother making this dish when she was a child living in Tregaron. Valmai has tried to recreate it, but alas, it never tastes quite the same.
I think this version is delicious, but no doubt Valmai and her mother would consider that my efforts lacked just a little something!
This can be served on its own or as an accompaniment to any meat.

SERVES 4

2 lb (1 kg) fresh parsnips, peeled and
   chopped
salt and freshly ground black pepper
1 oz (25 g) butter

2 oz (50 g) Welsh farmhouse Cheddar
   cheese, grated
3 tablespoons cream

1   Cook the parsnips in as little water as possible (the microwave is ideal for this); mash the soft parsnip, then add seasoning to taste and the butter. Stir in the grated cheese.

2   Just before serving pour over the cream and toast the parsnip under the grill.

LITTLE LEEK TARTS

*'There is a delicious cream-coloured cheese named after the town of Caerphilly in
South Wales,' to quote H. V. Morton from In Search of Wales, written in 1932 –
and certainly Caerphilly makes all the difference to these Little Leek Tarts.
You could use the ingredients to make one large leek flan, but I suggest that for a
change you prepare a batch of these tiny, tasty tarts. They keep well in the freezer, so
the next time you pack a picnic and head for a day on the hills you can take a
handful with you.
Remember that with a bite-sized pie it is really important to make sure that the filling
has lots of flavour, otherwise you are left with a rather dull mouthful of crumbs!*

SERVES 4

For the shortcrust pastry:
8 oz (225 g) plain flour
pinch of salt
5 oz (150 g) Welsh butter (salted)
1 egg yolk
water to mix

For the filling:
4 oz (100 g) smoked bacon (optional)

3 medium leeks, washed and finely sliced
1 oz (25 g) butter
8 oz (225 g) farmhouse Caerphilly cheese,
   grated
¼ pint (150 ml) dry white wine
2 tablespoons fresh cream
3 eggs
salt and freshly ground black pepper

1 Pre-heat the oven to gas mark 6, 400°F (200°C).

2 For the pastry, place flour and salt in a bowl; cut the butter into small pieces and rub into the flour.

3 Beat the egg yolk with a little water and pour into a well made in the centre of the flour mixture. Bind together until a dough is formed, adding more water if necessary.

4 Grease tartlet cases (or a large flan case if you prefer) and line each one with pastry. Bake 'blind' until the pastry is just firm but not coloured.

5 Re-set the oven to gas mark 4, 350°F (180°C).

6 For the filling, derind and dice the bacon and fry with the leeks in the butter until soft. Put a little of the mixture in the base of each tartlet. Divide the grated cheese and sprinkle on top of the leeks.

7 Boil the wine in a small saucepan until it is reduced by half, then leave to cool.

8 In a bowl whisk together the reduced wine, cream and eggs. Season well with salt and pepper, and pour the mixture over each tartlet.

9 Bake them for 15–20 minutes until they are puffed and golden.

10 Serve warm or cold.

COURGETTES WITH SAFFRON AND SOUR CREAM

Ancient Welsh medicine, a heady mixture of the down-to-earth and the mystical, was collated in the thirteenth century by members of a family known as the Physicians of Myddfai in Dyfed. One of their recommendations was to encourage merriment by eating saffron, though not too much 'for fear to die of mirth'!
Saffron is a pricy spice but a little goes a long way. The flavour is pungent and rather exotic and the superb golden yellow colour of this sauce will brighten up all sorts of dishes, from a bowl of sautéed courgettes to plain roast chicken or even poached white fish.

SERVES 4

2 lb (1 kg) firm smallish courgettes	½ pint (300 ml) chicken or fish stock
1 oz (25 g) butter	pinch of saffron
1 tablespoon shallot or onion, finely	salt and pepper
chopped	2 tablespoons sour cream
1 tablespoon flour	

1 Trim and slice the courgettes. Boil or steam them until cooked but not mushy.

2 Melt the butter in a small saucepan and cook the shallot very gently for 3 minutes without allowing it to brown. Add the flour and stir until blended. Cook for 1 minute.

3 Heat the stock and pour it on; stir until blended and simmer for 3–4 minutes, adding the saffron and salt and pepper to taste.

4 Stir in the sour cream.

YOGHURT CHEESE WITH FRESH HERBS

There is something very satisfying about making your own soft cheese. By straining the yoghurt you will be left with a sharp, thick, creamy mixture to mix with garlic and herbs. If you prefer a less tart flavour, use Greek-style yoghurt. Whether you serve it as a dip, rolled into pancakes or spread on crispbread, yoghurt cheese is a most useful ingredient to have in the fridge.

SERVES 4

1 pint (600 ml) natural yoghurt
freshly ground black pepper
1 tablespoon thin cream or top of the milk
½ clove garlic, crushed with salt

½ tablespoon chopped parsley
½ tablespoon chopped dill
½ tablespoon chopped chervil

1   Line a colander or strainer with muslin or a clean J-cloth and stand it over a bowl. Tip the yoghurt into the sieve and tie it up with string so that it forms a bag. Lift it out of the colander and leave it to drain overnight, tying the string to a tap over a sink.

2   The next day, tip the drained curds from the bag into a bowl. Beat until smooth, adding pepper and the cream or top of the milk.

3   Fold in the crushed garlic with most of the chopped herbs, keeping some back to scatter over the top.

4   Pile into a small dish, level off with a knife, and sprinkle the remaining herbs on top. Chill for an hour or two before serving.

CASSEROLE OF LEEKS WITH CREAM AND PARSLEY

This is a rich dish which could be served on its own with some chunks of fresh granary bread or as a moist vegetable casserole with a roast joint. It is particularly attractive with the green of the leeks peeping through the crisp brown cheesy topping.
For diet-minded cooks, an alternative to the cream could be creamy Greek-style yoghurt or some well-flavoured stock mixed with a tablespoonful of fresh brown breadcrumbs.

SERVES 4–6

2 lb (1 kg) leeks, slim and young if
  possible
2 tablespoons chopped parsley
good pinch of grated nutmeg
salt and black pepper

1 oz (25 g) butter
¼ pint (150 ml) fresh double cream
4–6 oz (100–175 g) grated Welsh
  farmhouse Cheddar-type cheese

1   Pre-heat the oven to gas mark 4, 350°F (180°C).

2   Slice the leeks into ½ inch (1 cm) lengths and wash well. Put them in a large ovenproof dish. Sprinkle the parsley over the leeks, add nutmeg and seasoning and dot with the butter. Place in the oven and cook for 15 minutes.

3   Pour the cream over the leeks and sprinkle with grated cheese.

4   Brown under a hot grill and serve at once with chunks of fresh granary bread.

POULTRY AND GAME

POULTRY

It wasn't so long ago that your mother might have swept the hearth with the tip of a goose wing. After all, everyone kept a goose in rural Wales, as much as an aggressor against unwanted visitors as for the table.

Geese, ducks and chickens were part of Welsh country life on a smallholding or farmyard. Did they taste better, I wonder, than the fresh yellow-fleshed corn-fed birds we can eat today? No doubt they had been scratching around building up their muscles, and few were eaten before their 'best date' in terms of maturity. Pot-roast or salt and stew were the normal poultry recipes for farmyard birds from the past. And I reckon a free-range farmyard bird would still be the one I'd choose if given the chance.

But we must not forget that chicken used to be expensive as well as tasty, and now we resent paying even 80p a pound for it. So can we expect to have good poultry for a song?

If you enjoy the relatively low price of poultry then you must expect to have to add flavours to it in the kitchen. Marinating poultry is very successful and portions of poultry can be pan-fried, microwaved or baked in a matter of minutes.

The flavour of smoked poultry is good, too, although the injecting of a smoky-flavoured saline solution into the bird doesn't appeal much to my saliva glands. However, if the flavour is reasonable and the danger of carcinogenic substances lessened then I'll go along with it!

GAME

Untamed Wales has always harboured a wealth of game which has been much enjoyed by rich and poor alike. Can't you just imagine the pleasure of a rabbit casserole or pigeon pie to brighten the rural family's dull and frugal diet?

Even in the cultivated areas the rule of the countryside deems it necessary to protect the crops from predators, be they rabbit, hare, pheasant, pigeon, grouse, woodcock or crow. Game is back in fashion, a meat for the nineties: lean, tasty, available and not too expensive.

The greatest problem with cooking game is knowing how to keep it moist. The lean, close texture of the flesh tends to become dry and hard very easily. Taking a lesson from Eileen Havard at the Griffin Inn at Llyswen in Powys, 'I find it best to pot-roast or casserole game, unless I know that a particular bird is very young.' Eileen cooks the breast of birds underneath to keep them moist, and adds lots of liquid to rabbit and hare.

Venison, traditionally bred in Hereford Forest, is now enjoying a revival in popularity. A farmed beast is very different from a well-hung, mature stag; it is tender and lean with a gamey but not overpowering flavour, and the top-grade cuts cook as quickly as steak.

DUCK WITH HONEY AND ORANGE

The last time I ate duck was with Ken Goody at his Cemlyn Restaurant in Harlech. No neat slices of duck breast with a dribble of sauce, but half a duckling filled my plate, encased in a crisp coat with the tender flesh literally falling off the bone. The sauce was sweet, spicy and deliciously tangy and I enjoyed every mouthful.

SERVES 4

5½ lb (2.5 kg) duck
4 tablespoons clear honey
2 tablespoons chopped thyme

the grated rind and juice of 2 oranges
salt and freshly ground black pepper

1 Pre-heat the oven to gas mark 6, 400°F (200°C).

2 Halve the duck and prick it here and there with a sharp skewer. Brush on both sides with honey. (If it is too thick, warm it slightly.)

3 Lay the duck, skin side uppermost, on an oiled roasting pan, and sprinkle with the chopped thyme, grated orange rind and some salt and black pepper. Pour over a little of the orange juice.

4 Leave for 1–2 hours to absorb the flavour, then bake in the oven for 50 minutes, basting with the remaining orange juice. Move the halves around once or twice, so that they brown evenly all over. They should be well browned, almost charred, on the outside, and nicely cooked inside.

5 To serve, cut the duck into quarters and lay them on a flat dish. Throw away the juice as it will be too fatty to serve with the duck.

6 Serve with rice, noodles or new potatoes and a green salad.

JUGGED HARE

In season from early autumn to the end of January, hare can be hung for up to 10 days – or even 14 days in cold weather. You may have seen them tied by the back legs to allow the blood to drain and collect in the thorax; this blood is used to thicken the gravy of jugged hare.

Indigenous to Wales, jugged hare is a dish that has been prepared since medieval times. The word jug means to cook, tightly covered, in a pot surrounded by hot water. By this method the close-textured flesh of the hare will cook entirely in its own juices and become tender. The blood of the hare is often added to the casserole at the end of cooking to thicken the juices and add a distinctive flavour. I don't always add it, though, since the sauce will curdle if boiled.

Ask the butcher to skin and joint the hare for you, adding some extra game bones for stock and keeping the blood if you want to include it in the sauce.

SERVES 4

1½–2 pints (900 ml–1.2 litres) game
   stock
2 oz (50 g) streaky bacon, chopped
2 oz (50 g) butter
1 hare, jointed
1 large onion, chopped
2 carrots, peeled and sliced

2 sticks celery
salt and freshly ground black pepper
bouquet garni
the finely grated rind of ½ lemon
1 oz (25 g) flour
4 tablespoons port
1 tablespoon redcurrant jelly

1   Pre-heat the oven to gas mark 2, 300°F (150°C).

2   Make up some good stock with the carcass bones from the hare and an onion, a carrot and some parsley stalks. Cover these with cold water, bring to the boil and simmer gently for 30 minutes. Strain the stock.

3   Fry the bacon in a deep, heavy-based casserole until the fat runs. Add the butter and fry the hare joints until well browned, then add the prepared vegetables, salt and pepper, bouquet garni and lemon rind. Pour over enough stock to cover the meat and bring to the boil.

4   Cover the pan tightly with a lid and cook in a cool oven for 2½–3 hours, or until tender.

5   Mix the flour to a smooth paste with a little water and stir it into the stew. Cook for a further 2–3 minutes.

6   Mix together the port, redcurrant jelly and hare's blood if wanted and carefully stir into the stew. Do not reheat the casserole but serve at once.

LADY LLANOVER'S SALT DUCK WITH ONION SAUCE

Lady Augusta Hall (Lady Llanover) made a great impression on the Welsh when she married Benjamin Hall, MP (after whom it is said Big Ben was named), and came to live in Abergavenny. She learnt to speak fluent Welsh and brought prosperity to many local people by opening a small woollens factory. In an effort to improve the moral character of her neighbours she bought and then closed all the local pubs, an act which did not endear her to many.

Don't be caught out in your preparations for her Salt Duck, for it takes three days to perfect. The salting process does wonders to the fattiness of a duck and the onion sauce gives it just the bite it needs. Altogether a very successful recipe, just one of many offered by Lady Llanover in her First Principles of Good Cookery, *written in 1867. Throughout this remarkable cookbook she narrates a fictional story in which the hero, a Welsh hermit, imparts all manner of cook's tips to a traveller who befriends him.*

SERVES 4

4–5 lb (1.75–2.25 kg) duck	2 fl oz (50 ml) water
4 oz (100 g) sea salt	1 level tablespoon plain flour
2 medium onions, chopped	½ pint (300 ml) milk

1   Rub the salt well into the flesh of the duck, turning and recoating the duck every day for 3 days.

2   Thoroughly rinse the salt off the duck and put it into a large pan or casserole. Pour over cold water to cover, bring to the boil and simmer very gently for 1½ hours, turning over halfway through.

3   Stew the chopped onion in the water very, very gently for about 15 minutes until tender.

4   Strain off the liquid, blend it with the flour using a whisk, add the milk and then return it to the onions. Bring the onion sauce to the boil. Simmer for a minute or two to cook the flour and thicken the sauce. Either liquidise or sieve the sauce, and taste for seasoning.

5   Serve the duck sliced with the sauce poured over it. Some colourful vegetables will brighten up the plate.

RABBIT IN WELSH MUSTARD AND THYME SAUCE

*Fresh rabbit has a fine flavour and firm texture and makes an inexpensive meal,
especially when served in a good sauce such as this recipe using mustard and thyme.
If you'd rather not tackle all that fur, why not ask your local fishmonger or game
supplier to skin and cut up your rabbit for you? For the squeamish there is always
frozen diced rabbit available in the supermarket.
Serve this dish with plenty of boiled potatoes or crusty french bread to mop up the
delicious sauce.*

SERVES 4

*1½ lb (750 g) jointed or boneless rabbit
seasoned flour
1 tablespoon sunflower oil
2 oz (50 g) butter
8 oz (225 g) pickling onions, peeled
2 cloves garlic, crushed with salt
1 tablespoon Welsh wholegrain mustard*

*½–¾ pint (300–450 ml) chicken stock
a good sprig of fresh thyme or ½ teaspoon
dried thyme
salt and pepper
¼ pint (150 ml) thick cream
fresh lemon juice (optional)*

1 Leave in joints, or cut the boneless rabbit into neat pieces, and roll in seasoned flour.

2 In a large, heavy-based casserole dish, heat the oil and butter and fry the rabbit until golden on all sides. Remove the rabbit and toss in the onions. Stir until lightly coloured all over, then add the garlic and cook for a further minute.

3 Stir in the mustard, pour on the stock and replace the rabbit. Add the thyme, salt and pepper. Cover the pan and cook very gently for 1½ hours, until tender, stirring occasionally.

4 Add the cream and stir until well blended; taste for seasoning, and add some fresh lemon juice to sharpen if necessary.

Mussels in a Savoury Choux Pastry Case, page 16.

Leek and Goat's Cheese Parcels, page 23.

Trout Wrapped in Bacon, page 35.

Yoghurt Cheese with Fresh Herbs, page 58.

Raised Game Pie, page 78.

Rack of Lamb with Mint Crust, page 90.

Summer Berry Pudding, page 104.

Barabrith and Welsh Cakes, page 115.

CHICKEN WITH WHINBERRY SAUCE

*Whinberries are of course myrtle berries, bilberries or blueberries. I have also used
fresh cranberries for this recipe.
Whinberry-picking is taken very seriously by the Welsh. Once the word is out that
the whinberries are ripe, then it's every man for himself, out on the open heathland.
Here is a recipe with the flavour of whinberries but without the calories and
cholesterol of a cream-laden whinberry tart.*

SERVES 4

4 large chicken breasts, skinned
1 tablespoon sunflower or other light
  cooking oil
1 oz (25 g) butter
¼ pint (150 ml) dry white wine

For the sauce:
8 oz (225 g) whinberries

4 tablespoons cold water
2 teaspoons honey
1 tablespoon raspberry or cider vinegar
salt and freshly ground pepper
lemon juice to taste
4 clusters of whinberries to garnish

1 Fry the chicken breasts gently in the oil and butter for 5 minutes.
Pour over the white wine, cover with a lid and simmer very gently for a
further 15–20 minutes.

2 Cook the fruit in the water until soft, then pour through a fine
sieve. Stir in the honey, vinegar and seasoning and adjust the sweet/
sour flavour of the sauce with lemon juice.

3 Pour a spoonful of the sauce on to each plate and arrange a sliced
chicken breast on top. Garnish with a cluster of fresh berries.

*Note: If you haven't made your own fruit vinegar before, then I suggest you start now
because it is very easy and most rewarding. Simply half-fill a jam jar or wide-necked
bottle with perfect unblemished fruit (raspberries are very good, but any berries will add
flavour to the vinegar). Now fill the bottle to the brim with good-quality white wine
vinegar and seal. Shake the bottle every day for a week, then strain the vinegar and add
it to fresh fruit for a second week. By this time the vinegar will have a fine fruity flavour
and become a useful addition to all kinds of recipes or salad dressings.*

CHICKEN AND HERB PARCELS

Both chicken and turkey meat could be used for this recipe. Dafydd Raw Rees from Borth near Aberystwyth would, of course, recommend the latter but only if you were able to use his fresh turkeys! 'The meat of the future' is how Dafydd sees turkeys: lean, inexpensive and an ideal vehicle for adding flavours.
By wrapping the poultry in greaseproof paper all the flavour is kept in and none of the moisture escapes. While the cream cheese adds a decadent richness to the chicken or turkey, the plain yoghurt will soften the flesh of the meat and the herbs add a fresh flavour.

SERVES 4

2 tablespoons wholegrain mustard
2 tablespoons cream cheese
1 tablespoon plain yoghurt
4 chicken breasts, or equivalent white turkey meat

salt and freshly ground black pepper
olive oil
2 tablespoons chopped lovage
1 tablespoon chopped parsley
juice of 1 lemon

1 Pre-heat the oven to gas mark 5, 375°F (190°C).

2 Mix the mustard with the cream cheese and yoghurt and coat the chicken pieces on all sides. Sprinkle with salt and pepper.

3 Brush 4 pieces of greaseproof paper with olive oil and lay the chicken breasts on them. Scatter a thick layer of herbs on top of each piece and sprinkle with lemon juice.

4 Wrap the paper round the breasts, folding the ends tightly so that no juice can escape. Place the envelopes on a baking sheet in the pre-heated oven for 30 minutes.

5 Serve the chicken wrapped in its paper case with jacket potatoes and a green salad.

CHICKEN WITH CIDER AND LOVAGE

Gone are the days when chickens pecked their way around the yard of most country homes in Wales. Free-range birds are still available, though, if you get to know the rural communities. Lovage has an unusual musky flavour, similar to celery, and together with the cider gives this dish a really good flavour.

SERVES 4

1 tablespoon rapeseed or groundnut oil
1 oz (25 g) butter
4 chicken breasts
¼ pint (150 ml) dry cider
1 tablespoon chopped lovage or chervil

1 tablespoon chopped sorrel, or the grated
rind of ½ lemon
salt and freshly ground black pepper
2 tablespoons fromage frais or Greek
yoghurt

1   Heat the oil and butter in a heavy-based casserole or large frying-pan until sizzling. Fry the chicken breasts, turning after 4 or 5 minutes, until golden brown on both sides.

2   Lower the heat and pour in the cider, add the chopped herbs and seasoning. Cover the pan with a lid and simmer the chicken for 15–20 minutes until cooked through.

3   Remove the chicken and arrange on a serving dish.

4   Add the fromage frais to the pan and stir well to mix with the cider juices. Pour this sauce over the chicken.

STICKY CHICKEN

The combination of fresh lemons, garlic and honey must make this the perfect chicken recipe. Easy, quick and delicious, I find that everyone likes it, from granny to the toddlers.
It is also a clever way to cook those convenient frozen chicken portions that we all fall prey to in times of stress!

SERVES 4

4 large or 8 small chicken portions
1 or 2 cloves garlic
2 tablespoons honey

the grated rind and juice of 2 lemons
salt and freshly ground black pepper

1   Arrange the chicken joints in an ovenproof dish.

2   Peel and crush the garlic cloves with a pinch of salt; warm the honey a little if it is stiff, then mix it with the garlic and lemon rind and juice. Season with salt and pepper. Pour this sticky mixture over the chicken and leave to marinate for at least 2 hours, stirring from time to time.

3   Pre-heat the oven to gas mark 5, 375°F (190°C).

4   Bake the chicken for 45 minutes to an hour, turning once so that both sides are crisp and brown. Test the chicken to make sure it is cooked through – no red juices should run when pierced with a sharp knife.

5   Serve the chicken in its own juices with jacket potatoes or crusty bread and freshly boiled beans or broccoli.

PIGEONS WITH SPICY PLUM SAUCE

Wood pigeons, plump on stolen corn, are delicious. They have lots of flesh and a good gamey flavour, but be sure to cover the breast with fat bacon if you roast them so that the lean flesh doesn't dry out.

SERVES 4

4 *pigeon breasts, plump and young*
4 *bay leaves*
4 *thick slices of orange*
8 *rashers streaky bacon*

For the sauce:
10 *cooking plums (or prunes, soaked overnight in orange juice)*
2 *medium onions, chopped*

3 *tablespoons olive oil*
3 *teaspoons fresh marjoram (or 1 teaspoon dried marjoram)*
1 *dessertspoon soy sauce*
½ *pint (300 ml) red wine*
the juice of 1 orange
salt and pepper

1 Pre-heat the oven to gas mark 6, 400°F (200°C).

2 Wash the pigeon breasts and put a bay leaf and a slice of orange into the cavity of each; lay two slices of bacon across each one, securing with cocktail sticks if necessary.

3 Put the pigeon breasts in a baking tin small enough to fit them snugly; add 2 tablespoons of water and roast for 30–40 minutes or until the juices run clean when pierced with a sharp knife. Keep warm.

4 Stone the plums or prunes and chop roughly.

5 Fry the onions gently in the oil until soft and add the plums, herbs, soy sauce, wine and some salt and pepper. Cook gently for about 15 minutes, until the sauce thickens.

6 Sieve and reheat, adding the orange juice just before serving in a sauce boat with the roast pigeon on a separate dish.

RAISED GAME PIE

Real pub food, this, just what you would expect if you stopped at the Griffin Inn for a bite. Eileen Havard, the cook, uses whatever game comes her way – pheasant, rabbit, hare, grouse, pigeon, venison and partridge – as well as some ham and chicken.

SERVES 4–6

For the filling:
1 pheasant, plucked and drawn
½ teaspoon thyme
2 bayleaves
1 level dessertspoon salt
24 black peppercorns
1 large carrot, chopped
1 stick celery, chopped
1 large onion, chopped
10 oz (275 g) assorted cooked meats,
  diced (i.e. chicken, ham, and whatever
  game is available)

¼ pint (150 ml) red wine
1 tablespoon mixed fresh herbs or 1
  teaspoon dried herbs

For the pastry case:
4½ oz (120 g) lard
¼ pint (150 ml) water
12 oz (350 g) plain flour
½ teaspoon salt
1 egg yolk
beaten egg to glaze

The filling must be prepared the day before you make the pie.

1   Put the pheasant in a large saucepan with the herbs, seasoning and chopped carrots, celery and onion. Add enough cold water to cover and bring to the boil; simmer until tender for about 90 minutes. Leave to cool in the liquid.

2   Strip the flesh from the pheasant carcass, and reserve the pheasant stock.

3   In a large bowl, combine the chopped pheasant with the other cooked meats. Pour over the red wine and stir in the fresh herbs. Cover and leave overnight in a cool place.

4   Pre-heat the oven to gas mark 6, 400°F (200°C).

5   Grease a loose-bottom 6 inch (15 cm) diameter tin and dust with flour.

6   Melt the fat over a gentle heat.

7   Bring the water to the boil, take off the heat and tip in the sieved flour with the salt. Stir well to combine, then make a well in the dough

and pour in the melted fat and the egg yolk. Beat hard to make a dough and knead into a smooth ball. Keep warm.

8   Roll out three-quarters of the pastry into a large circle and line the tin.

9   Spoon the prepared filling into the case.

10   Roll out the remaining pastry to make a lid and seal the edges with cold water. Design a pattern on the lid if you like and make a ¼ inch (5 mm) hole in the centre. Glaze with beaten egg.

11   Bake for 15 minutes, then turn the oven down to gas mark 3, 325°F (160°C) for another 60–90 minutes.

12   Meanwhile, reheat the pheasant stock and boil hard to reduce to about ½ pint (300 ml). Pour the warm stock through the hole in the cooked pie, until full. Leave to cool.

13   Serve the raised game pie cut into slices, with a side salad and relishes.

PHEASANT WITH SAGE AND APPLES

Pheasants are to be found in such number in Clwyd, particularly in the Ceiriog Forest near Llangollen, that they look quite indignant as cars approach to clutter up their roads!
A glut of pheasants means of course the price comes down and even if you don't live near a poulterer, most supermarkets now sell dressed pheasant during the season. The cheapest way to buy pheasants is fully feathered but they need to be hung for about a week in a cool place and plucking a well-hung pheasant is not easy for the skin is soft and tears easily.

SERVES 4

½ pint (300 ml) good game stock
1 tablespoon sunflower seed oil
2 oz (50 g) butter
2 plump pheasants
1 large onion, chopped
¼ pint (150 ml) Calvados and dry cider
  mixed

4–5 Cox's apples, peeled, cored and sliced
1 tablespoon fresh sage, chopped
1 bayleaf
salt and freshly ground black pepper
½ pint (300 ml) thick cream

1 Ask the butcher for any gamey bits and pieces he has suitable for stock – perhaps a pheasant carcass – and add this to a pan of cold water with half an onion, some parsley stalks, a diced carrot and a stick of celery. Bring to the boil and simmer for 20 minutes, no longer or it may become bitter. Leave to cool, then strain the game stock.

2 Heat the oil and butter in a heavy-based casserole large enough to take both pheasants. Fry the pheasants so that they brown on all sides. Lift them out and fry the onion until soft and golden. Pour in the cider and Calvados. Let it boil until it has reduced by half its volume.

3 Pour in the stock, add the apples, herbs and seasoning and bring to the boil. Replace the pheasants, cover tightly and simmer gently for about 50 minutes. The pheasants will be cooked when the leg feels as though it will come away easily from the body.

4 Remove the pheasants from the casserole, carve and arrange in a serving dish.

5 Strain the casserole juices, pressing the contents well so that the apples and onions pass through the sieve, and return the sauce to the pan. Add the cream and bring to the boil. Season to taste, adding a little more Calvados or perhaps a squeeze of lemon juice to sharpen, and pour the sauce over the pheasant.

6   Serve with mashed potato which has been cooked with celery.

VENISON STEAK WITH JUNIPER BERRIES

Venison is becoming increasingly popular in Wales, although it is hardly a new phenomenon. Friends in Brecon remember enjoying venison before the Second World War; for a little over £1 they could buy a fine piece of venison haunch in the market, sold off after the deer cull in the Hereford Forest.
A cull will bring in the old deer and this is why we think of venison as a gamey, tough meat, but the venison we eat today is nearly always less than two and a half years old. With the ever-increasing supply of venison from deer farms, we are in the luxurious position of having a choice between tender young venison with its own highly distinctive flavour, and game venison which has been hung for a longer period.

SERVES 4

4 × 6 oz (175 g) venison loin steaks
1 tablespoon juniper berries, crushed
2 tablespoons sunflower or any light
  cooking oil
2 oz (50 g) butter

4 tablespoons gin
the grated rind and juice of 1 orange
1 tablespoon redcurrant jelly
salt and freshly ground black pepper
3 tablespoons double cream

1   Put the venison steaks between two pieces of greaseproof paper and beat until they are thin. Brush them with a very little oil and press the crushed juniper berries on to them.

2   Heat the oil and butter in a large frying-pan and sear the chops on both sides over a fierce heat. Turn the heat down and continue to cook the venison until it is as you like it. Remove the steaks from the pan.

3   Pour in the gin and allow it to bubble up and reduce by half its volume. Add the orange juice and rind, redcurrant jelly and seasoning. Bring the sauce to the boil and take off the heat.

4   Stir in the cream and pour at once over the steaks. Serve immediately.

MEAT

LAMB

Lamb is the meat of Wales, of this there is no doubt, and it is the best! But why is it so good? Because it's natural. Think of those sheep grazing on the windswept Welsh mountains or moorland; you can be sure that no farmer is feeding them complex feedstuffs up there. And if they take longer to mature to a good size, won't the flavour be better?

Welsh mountain sheep are a special hardy breed who have particularly good mothering qualities and produce lambs with a proper wool coat to begin life on the hillside. They may not produce as many lambs as other breeds and their wool is poor, so many sheep farmers now cross-breed their sheep to get the best quality beasts. The mixture of breeds varies throughout Wales: in mid-Wales you will find a Welsh Mountain crossed perhaps with a Blue-Horn Leicester; on the Brecon Beacons the sheep will be a cross between a Welsh Mountain and a Cheviot.

Lowland lamb is different again, for it needn't be so hardy and must mature quickly to reach the dinner table in time for Easter. Often these sheep are a cross between Welsh Mountain and Hereford or Charolais. Is there then any truth in the ditty:

> Mountain lamb is sweet
> Valley lamb is fatter
> I therefore deemed it meet
> to carry off the latter!

The truth is that top-quality lamb is available all the year round now, with lowland spring lamb ready for Easter, continuing on until the mountain lamb reaches the shops in August.

Lamb is lean too, for the butchers know that the housewife won't buy fat meat any more. Organisations such as Welsh Lamb Enterprise, who grade and promote the meat, advise farmers as to the quality they must breed their sheep. Sold on the hoof, a lamb can become too fat in a matter of days and so lose the farmer a premium price.

New cuts of lamb are making it a convenience food; with most of the bones removed with the fat it is a much easier meat to cook.

Franco and Ann Taruschio serve local lamb throughout the year at the Walnut Tree Restaurant near Abergavenny. Trimming a loin, Franco prepared chops and served them with polenta, wild mushrooms and a timbale of leeks and parma ham for the TV series. His combination of Welsh and Italian ingredients complement each other superbly.

PORK

The fat family bacon pig is alas a thing of the past. At one time every rural home in Wales had a pig or two. Killed in the autumn, the fresh meat was distributed between friends and neighbours; hams were brined, salted, cured or smoked, thus ensuring that they lasted through the winter to feed the family. Fed on grain and swill, the pig was a thoroughly useful addition to a rural household.

But today good health sense tells us that we don't need such quantities of animal fat in our diet, and pigs are bred to be long, thin and lean. The diet, lifestyle and growth programme of a modern pig factory is something I'd rather not dwell on. But Tony Evans, with his Sker Free Range Meat Company in Porthcawl, produces traditional pork without charging a lot more for it.

BEEF

The Welsh Black has a wonderful flavour, but for the modern farmer it is too small, has too much fat marbled into the meat and matures too slowly. So most beef farmers now cross-breed their hardy Welsh Blacks with Continental breeds such as Charolais or Limosin. These large-frame cows give lean meat and lots of it and they also grow fast.

Lean beef at a reasonable price is what we want, isn't it? Or is it? Since most of us have cut down on our meat consumption, why not spoil ourselves with something a little tastier? Cut off the fat round the edge and enjoy the tenderness of a steak that has natural marbling through it. But it will, of course, cost more.

And who convinced us that we want bright pink meat? What about protem? This is an enzyme found in papayas, which is injected into the live beast just before slaughter. It activates an early breakdown of the tissues so that the meat will become tender without the traditional week or so of hanging. Does the housewife know about this? Does she care? Or is a bright pink piece of meat at a good price all she's interested in?

Someone who certainly knows his beef is David Barrett, the chef at Tyddyn Llan Hotel in Llandrillo near Corwen. Bridget Kindred, owner of the hotel, buys the best local Welsh Black beef and David leaves it to hang for up to three weeks in his cold room. 'People seem to have forgotten how to chew,' says Bridget, 'so we always offer tender fillet steak on the menu, but sirloin must be the best for flavour.'

BONELESS SHOULDER OF LAMB WITH GINGER, HONEY, CIDER AND ROSEMARY

John Morgan, a helpful butcher in Cardiff Market, first showed me how to bone out a shoulder and remove the unwanted fat that lurks behind the bone. A simple process, which most butchers are happy to perform, and which gives a lean joint that is easy to carve. As John says, a boned, rolled shoulder will feed more mouths than cutting a roast off the bone.

SERVES 4

1 shoulder of lamb, weighing about 3 lb
(1.5 kg) with the bone
2 cloves garlic, crushed with salt
1 inch (2.5 cm) piece fresh ginger, peeled
and finely grated
1 oz (25 g) butter, melted

2 tablespoons honey
1 tablespoon rosemary, spikes rather than
ground, fresh if possible
3½ fl oz (100 ml) cider
salt and freshly ground pepper

1 Pre-heat the oven to gas mark 6, 400°F (200°C).

2 Lay the boned shoulder of lamb, skin side down, on a clean work surface. Spread the crushed garlic and grated ginger over the lamb and fold over into a tidy roll. Sew or tie to keep in shape.

3 Mix the butter, honey and rosemary together. Spread this over the skin of the lamb. Cover the lamb loosely with tinfoil, shiny side outwards, and sit the joint in a roasting tin. Add the cider.

4 Roast in a moderately hot oven, allowing 15–20 minutes to the pound. Halfway through cooking, remove the foil, and continue cooking, basting frequently with juices from the roasting tin.

5 Remove the joint from the oven and allow to cool slightly.

6 Strain the juices from the pan, removing any excess fat, and pour in a little cider to 'deglaze' the pan. Boil fiercely, then return the non-fatty juices to the pan and thicken the sauce with a little arrowroot or kneaded butter. (To make kneaded butter, mix 1 oz (25 g) softened butter and a tablespoon of plain flour together on a work surface with a palette knife).

7   Boil well to disperse the lumps and season to taste.

I think that kneaded butter thickens a sauce to give it a good glossy finish, much superior to cornflour or arrowroot. Keep any extra kneaded butter in the fridge.

LAMB AND LEEK STIR-FRY

As with all stir-fry dishes, the ingredients for this recipe must be of top quality because they are cooked for such a short time. For the lamb I recommend neck fillet if possible, but best end of neck or loin will work well as long as the fat is cut off.

SERVES 4

1½ lb (750 g) lamb neck fillet or best end of neck or loin, with fat removed
1½ inch (4 cm) piece fresh ginger, peeled
1 clove garlic, crushed with salt
2 tablespoons dry sherry
1 tablespoon cornflour

freshly ground black pepper
3 small leeks, trimmed and washed
1 large spear broccoli
2 carrots, peeled
4 tablespoons vegetable oil

1   Cut the lamb into very thin slices and put in a bowl. Shred or grate the ginger and add to the lamb with the garlic, sherry and cornflour. Season well with pepper. Mix and leave to stand while preparing the vegetables.

2   Slice the leeks thinly; cut the broccoli into small florets, cut the carrots into matchsticks.

3   Heat half of the oil in a wok or large frying-pan. Add half of the lamb and marinade ingredients and stir-fry for 2 minutes. In order to keep the heat high and stir-fry the lamb correctly I suggest that you either use two woks or large frying-pans or cook the lamb in two batches.

4   Add half of the prepared vegetables and cook for 2 to 3 minutes until tender but still crisp.

5   Serve immediately.

FRANCO TARUSCHIO'S WELSH LAMB WITH WILD MUSHROOMS AND POLENTA

No one has won more accolades for good food in Wales than Franco Taruschio at the
Walnut Tree Inn near Abergavenny, and his immensely high standards have been
maintained for over 25 years. Franco and his wife Ann opened the Walnut Tree
while on their honeymoon, serving just one table and offering honest fresh local food
with an Italian flavour. They delighted their diners then as they do now. Some of the
very first customers still return to eat lasagne at the bar!
In this recipe Franco has combined Welsh lamb with leeks, parma ham, polenta and
wild mushrooms. He suggests that if possible you should go hunting for wild
mushrooms, but if not then look in good supermarkets or greengrocers who should
offer a good range. Look for oyster mushrooms, cepes, chanterelles, pièds de mouton
or any others available. Use a mixture or only one variety.
Polenta is a kind of maize flour porridge. Nowadays an instant form of polenta flour
is available.
Although this recipe sounds rather complicated, taken stage by stage it should not
overstretch you. For the finished dish, 3 double lamb chops are arranged on each
individual plate and to accompany them a spoonful of wild mushrooms, a mound of
shredded leek and parma ham and some diamonds of polenta. The sauce is a
reduction of the basic lamb stock.

SERVES 4

For the sauce:
trimmings of the carre (rack or best end)
  of lamb
1 large onion, roughly chopped
4 medium carrots, chopped
3 sticks celery, chopped
2 bay leaves
4 fl oz (120 ml) Marsala
1 tablespoon tomato purée
1½ pints (900 ml) water
6 cloves garlic
sprig of rosemary

4 best ends of Welsh lamb (each strip with
  6 chops)
olive oil
2 eggs, beaten
4 oz (100 g) fresh breadcrumbs
1 tablespoon thyme
1 tablespoon parsley
1 tablespoon marjoram
salt and pepper

Garnishes:

a) Wild mushrooms: toss 8 oz (225 g) wild mushrooms in hot olive oil.

b) Leek and parma ham: sweat 3 finely chopped shallots gently in
1 tablespoon olive oil and ½ oz (15 g) butter till soft. Add the white
parts of 6 leeks cut into julienne strips and cook until softened. Add
2 oz (50 g) parma ham, finely shredded, and salt and pepper. (Go
carefully with the salt as the ham is already salty.)

c) Fried polenta: salt and bring to the boil 1¾ pints (1 litre) of water; slowly add 9 oz (250 g) instant polenta flour, stirring constantly until you have a thick paste. Remove from the heat and after 1 minute turn out on to a lightly oiled tin or plate. When cold cut into diamond shapes. Fry the polenta in a little olive oil till golden and crispy to serve with the lamb.

For the sauce:

1   Brown the trimmings of the carre or best end of lamb in a roasting tin in a hot oven; drain off nearly all the fat and remove the bones to a saucepan. Add the onion, carrots, celery and bay leaves to the roasting tin and brown well, then pour in the Marsala, allow to bubble till well reduced, then add the tomato purée and stir.

2   Add the water, scraping well round the roasting tin. Add the contents of the roasting tin to the bones in the saucepan with the garlic and rosemary. Bring to boil and simmer for 1½–2 hours, skimming frequently.

3   Sieve, and return the sauce to the stove and reduce to a smooth consistency.

For the meat:

4   Pre-heat the oven to gas mark 8, 450°F (230°C).

5   Seal the lamb in hot oil in a roasting tin, then remove and brush the outer surface with the beaten egg and cover with the breadcrumbs mixed with the herbs and seasoning, pressing well to bind the crumbs.

6   Return the lamb to the roasting tin and cook in the oven for about 7 minutes or until the meat is pink. Remove from the oven and leave to rest for 4 minutes.

7   While the meat is resting, fry the mushrooms for the garnish in oil and salt and pepper to taste.

8   Carve the meat into 3 double chops per person. Put the sauce on to the plates and place the chops to one side. Garnish with a mound of mushrooms, a mound of leek and parma ham and 3 diamonds of fried polenta. Decorate with a tiny sprig of thyme.

LAMB STEAK WITH ROWAN AND ORANGE JELLY

'Invitation to Paradise', says the brochure to Hafod Lodge at Cwmystwyth.
Remembering the comfort of the lodge, and the welcome I got there, I can say that I
felt happily trapped inside its pearly gates. Colin and Jenny Beard are perfect hosts
and their attention to detail is second to none. With a maximum capacity of 12 for a
meal, and three double rooms upstairs for lucky travellers, visitors may expect to feel
spoilt.
Jenny says that she prefers to cook Welsh mountain lamb in early autumn when it is
lean and succulent from summer grazing on the local hills.
Redcurrant jelly may be the traditional accompaniment to serve with spring lamb,
but autumn lamb tastes great with jelly made from the eye-catching bright red
rowanberries which abound on the mountains from September.

SERVES 4

For the jelly:
3 lb (1.5 kg) rowanberries, picked over
 and washed
3 lb (1.5 kg) crab apples, sliced
zest and juice of 3 oranges

light soft brown sugar
a few drops of orange flower water

4 × 6 oz (175 g) premium leg steaks of
 Welsh mountain lamb
1 tablespoon hazelnut oil

1   Put the berries, apples and zest and juice of the oranges in a saucepan and cover with water. Simmer till pulpy, then strain through a jelly bag.

2   Measure the liquid and for every pint (600 ml) of juice add 1 lb (450 g) of soft brown sugar. Add the orange flower water.

3   Dissolve the sugar slowly, stirring all the time, then bring to the boil and boil hard till setting point is reached.

4   Pour into clean, warm, dry jars and seal.

5   Brush the steaks with the hazelnut oil and pre-heat the grill or a heavy non-stock frying-pan. Grill or fry the steaks over high heat to crisp on both sides.

6   Turn the heat down a little and continue to cook the meat through until it is as you like it.

7   Serve the lamb straight from the pan with some crisp fresh vegetables and the sharp almost smoky-flavoured rowan and orange jelly.

NOISETTES OF LAMB WITH LAVER AND ORANGE SAUCE

'A capital dinner! you don't get moor mutton, with hot laver sauce every day!' –
Collins, 1875.
Is this dish the epitome of Welsh food? Tender Welsh lamb served with a sauce of
Pembrokeshire seaweed. The sauce has a rich flavour of the sea with a not
unpleasant glutinous texture that benefits from a good squeeze of fruit juice to
sharpen it. Fresh or tinned laverbread will work well for the sauce but if neither is
available then use a purée of spinach and add a few drops of anchovy essence.

SERVES 4

8 oz (225 g) laverbread
grated rind and juice of ½ orange
juice of ½ lemon
1 oz (25 g) butter

salt and freshly ground black pepper
8–12 noisettes of lamb, neatly tied, with a
thin surround of fat or 4 Valentine lamb
steaks

1   In a small pan heat the laverbread and fruit juice. Cook for a few minutes, stirring all the time, then add the butter, little by little until the sauce looks rich and glossy. Season to taste and keep warm.

2   Heat the grill to its hottest and cook the noisettes or steaks, turning once, until they are crisp on the outside but still a little pink in the middle.

3   Serve the lamb with the sauce separately and a mixture of mashed root vegetables such as carrot and parsnip or swede to offset the colour of the laverbread sauce.

Rack of Lamb with Mint Crust

Twenty to 30 minutes is all it takes to roast a rack of lamb. Ask the butcher to prepare your joint so that the rib bones are scraped clean at the end and the sinew has been cut away from the base. By chining the lamb the butcher will cut the backbone away from the ribs. All you need to do is heat a pretty hot oven and press this tasty mint crust on to the meat.
To serve, simply cut down between the rib chops and give two or three per person; they should be just a little pink in the middle.

Serves 3–4

3 tablespoons soft white breadcrumbs
3 tablespoons mint sauce
1 tablespoon chopped parsley
1 clove garlic, crushed with salt
salt and freshly ground black pepper
1 egg white
1½–2 lb (750–1 kg) best end of neck of lamb, skinned and chined (you may need to roast two best end pieces if they are from a small Welsh lamb)

For the mint sauce:
2 tablespoons chopped fresh mint
1 tablespoon honey, dissolved in 2 tablespoons boiling water
1 dessertspoon raspberry vinegar

1 Pre-heat the oven to gas mark 7, 425°F (220°C).

2 Make up the mint sauce by mixing the chopped mint with the honey, boiling water and raspberry vinegar.

3 Mix the breadcrumbs to a paste with the mint sauce, adding the chopped parsley and the finely chopped garlic. Add salt and pepper to taste and bind together with the egg white.

4 Score the surface of the lamb with a sharp knife and spread the mint crust over, pressing it down well with a palette knife.

5 Put the rack of lamb in a roasting tin and cook in the hot oven for 20–30 minutes, depending on how pink you like your lamb. Baste once during the roasting time with the pan juices and return to the oven to finish cooking. The crust should be golden brown when the cooking time is up.

6 Serve the roast rack of lamb with redcurrant jelly.

PORK CHOPS WITH HONEY, SAGE AND HAZELNUTS

Here is a quick and easy recipe that tastes great as long as all the ingredients are top quality. Pure local honey, fresh sage and newly cracked hazelnuts make a good blend of flavours with the pork.
Rely on a good butcher for your pork chops; nothing is worse than tough pork. The honey will sweeten the meat and the hazelnut oil will keep it moist, but be sure to baste the chops often during grilling so that they don't dry out.

SERVES 4

3 tablespoons clear honey
3 tablespoons chopped fresh sage
1 tablespoon chopped fresh parsley
1 tablespoon ground hazelnuts

1 tablespoon hazelnut oil
juice of ½ lemon
salt and pepper
4 good-sized pork chops

1 In a bowl mix the honey, herbs, nuts, oil, lemon juice and seasoning. (If the honey is thick, it should be slightly warmed.)

2 Heat the grill to its hottest and arrange the chops on a grill pan. Cook them on one side and then turn them over.

3 Spread the mixture across the uncooked side of the chops and replace under the grill until the mixture caramelises.

4 If the chops are thick, finish cooking in a moderate oven for 10 minutes.

5 Serve immediately, with new potatoes and a green salad.

FILLET OF PORK WITH CARAMELISED APPLES

Pork tenderloin has very little fat, an excellent flavour and cooks quickly. Although it is an expensive cut, it suits the busy cook who likes to prepare quality meals in a minimum of time. The caramelised apples and cider add a rich stickiness to this dish which I love.

SERVES 4

1½ lb (750 g) pork tenderloin
1 tablespoon olive oil
1 oz (25 g) butter
1 large onion, sliced
¼ pint (150 ml) dry cider
salt and freshly ground black pepper

For the garnish:
2 red-skinned eating apples
1 oz (25 g) butter
2 teaspoons sugar
1 tablespoon dry cider

1 Slice the pork tenderloin into ½ inch (1 cm) discs, cutting slightly on the diagonal.

2 Heat the oil and butter in a large frying-pan and fry the pork, a few pieces at a time, until browned on both sides. The oil will stop the butter from burning so you can maintain a good heat while frying the pork. Remove the meat from the pan.

3 Add the sliced onion and cook until it softens, then pour in the cider, stirring well to loosen any sediment from the bottom of the pan. Season.

4 Return the pork to the pan, lower the heat, cover and simmer for 15 minutes.

5 Transfer the pork to a serving dish, pour over the sauce and wipe out the frying-pan.

6 Quarter and core the apples, but leave the skins on. Heat the remaining butter, and when it sizzles slice the apples straight into the pan. Stir continuously until the apple slices are well coated with butter.

7 Sprinkle in the sugar and continue to toss the apples till they brown. Remove them before they break up.

8   Arrange the apple slices over the pork, add the extra tablespoon of cider to the pan, stir well and then pour over the apples.

9   Serve with fresh vegetables – perhaps a purée of potatoes and celeriac and sprouts dusted with nutmeg.

BABS WEBB'S FAGGOTS

As a teenage girl Babs was in service to a wealthy family with a large house near her home in Llandeilo, in Dyfed. There she picked up the basis of good cooking, a skill she used throughout her busy life as a farmer's wife with four children. Today, outside the back door of her pretty retirement cottage, she has a neat row of herbs which she uses daily: sage for pork, mint and rosemary for lamb, savory for casseroles and, of course, basil to keep the flies away.
Here is Babs' delicious country recipe for faggots, an all-time favourite dish for the Welsh, who always serve them with gravy and peas.

MAKES BETWEEN 25 AND 30 FAGGOTS

1 lb (450 g) pork liver
8 oz (225 g) pigs' lights, pipes cut out
12 oz (350 g) spleen
12 oz (350 g) heart
12 oz (350 g) fresh lean pork
2 cooking apples, peeled, cored and
*   chopped*

2 medium onions, chopped
4 thick slices wholemeal bread, crumbed
1 teaspoon mixed herbs (sage, thyme,
*   savory, parsley and rosemary)*
salt and pepper
caul or veil

1   Pre-heat the oven to gas mark 4, 350°F (180°C).

2   In a large pan combine the liver, lights, spleen, heart and fresh pork. Cover with water and simmer for an hour. Leave to cool in the liquid, then chop or mince everything. Keep the juices.

3   Mix the apples, onions, breadcrumbs, herbs and seasoning into the meat, adding about half of the liquid to make a good moist mixture. Shape into handful-sized balls.

4   Cut the caul or veil into squares and wrap around each faggot. Pack them into a large baking tray. Alternatively, spread a layer of caul over the bottom of the baking tray, fill in the faggots and spread more caul over the top.

5   Bake in the oven for 1–1½ hours.

BEEF AND PORK PARCELS IN RED WINE

Margaret Rees remembers her mother making this dish, and she still serves it today in her restaurant, The Cobblers at Llandybie. The French call these cork-shaped beef rolls alouettes sans têtes *(larks without heads), and they are so tasty it might be difficult to decipher exactly what ingredients go into them. Rest assured, it isn't larks! The parcels are rather a fiddle to prepare but the finished dish is well worth the effort.*

SERVES 4

1½ lb (750 g) topside, sliced very thinly
2 rounded teaspoons French mustard
salt and freshly ground black pepper
4 oz (100 g) streaky bacon, diced
1 medium onion, chopped
4 oz (100 g) field mushrooms, chopped
4 oz (100 g) lean pork, minced
1 large clove garlic, crushed with salt
2 oz (50 g) wholemeal breadcrumbs
1 egg
1 tablespoon chopped parsley
2 tablespoons sherry

For the sauce:
1 large onion, sliced
1 large carrot, diced
1 stick celery, sliced
1½ oz (40 g) beef dripping or lard
½ pint (300 ml) beef stock
¼ pint (150 ml) red wine
1 oz (25 g) butter kneaded with 1 oz
   (25 g) plain flour, or arrowroot or
   cornflour

1   Pre-heat the oven to gas mark 3, 325°F (160°C).

2   Beat the beef slices wafer-thin between two pieces of waxed paper: each slice should measure about 4 × 4 inches (10 ×10 cm). Spread a little mustard over each slice; season with salt and freshly ground black pepper.

3   Dry-fry the bacon until the fat runs, add the onion and mushrooms and cook gently for 5 minutes. Leave to cool.

4   Mix the bacon, onion, mushrooms, minced pork, garlic, breadcrumbs, egg, parsley and sherry. Spoon the stuffing equally on the beef slices; roll up each slice and tuck the ends over to keep the stuffing in place. Tie each paupiette securely with fine string.

5   Fry the onion, carrot and celery over moderate heat in the beef dripping in the bottom of a heavy-based casserole. Allow the vegetables to brown slightly before placing the paupiettes in a neat row on top of the vegetables. Pour in the stock and wine and cover the casserole. Cook in the pre-set oven for 1¾ hours, turning the meat once during cooking.

6   Lift the paupiettes from the casserole, remove the string and arrange the meat on a warm serving dish. Strain the cooking liquid into a small saucepan and boil rapidly to reduce the sauce by a third.

7   Thicken the sauce with kneaded butter or arrowroot and spoon a little of the sauce over the meat, serving the rest in a sauce boat.

8   Serve with buttered noodles or creamed potatoes.

WELSH BEEF WITH POTATO AND ONION GALETTE SERVED WITH ASPARAGUS AND A PORT WINE SAUCE

At Tyddyn Llan Country House Hotel at Llandrillo near Corwen, David Barrett insists on local Welsh Black beef. His local butcher obliges in every way except to hang it long enough to satisfy David.
'I like my beef to hang for at least 14 days so that the flesh is tender and the flavour more pronounced.'
The beef is marbled with fat which helps to keep it moist and gives it that extra flavour. David cuts off fat from the edge of the steaks just before he sends the plates out of the kitchen, but he leaves it there for the cooking so that it too gives the meat extra flavour.
Fresh beef stock is now available in supermarkets and makes a good alternative to making your own if you don't have the time.
David likes to serve this elegant dish accompanied by a small tartlet of leeks and laverbread and a selection of fresh vegetables served separately.

SERVES 4

For the stock:
12 oz (350 g) carrots, chopped
4 medium onions, sliced
1 leek, sliced
4 sticks celery, sliced
1 oxtail (approx 1 lb 10 oz (800 g), chopped into rings
3 chicken carcasses (free from butcher), chopped into 3 parts
2 tablespoons honey
6 pints (3.5 litres) water
5 oz (150 g) tomato purée
4 stalks parsley
6 sage leaves

2 large old potatoes
1 small onion
salt and freshly ground black pepper
2 egg yolks
2 tablespoons olive oil
16 (1 bunch) asparagus spears
4 × 8 oz (225 g) prime sirloin steaks or 4 × 6 oz (175 g) fillet steaks (when using sirloin choose thick steaks rather than the larger thin ones)
2 fl oz (50 ml) port or good red wine
1 oz (25 g) butter

The stock must be made at least a day in advance and can be stored in the fridge for a few days or frozen. It can be used as the base for many meat sauces; you can make a large quantity and freeze it in small amounts for use later. Do not use stock cubes as an easy alternative for this dish as they have a very high salt content and cannot be reduced.

1 Pre-heat the oven to gas mark 4, 350°F (180°C).

2   Put the vegetables in a roasting tin and put the oxtail and chicken carcasses on top, brushed with honey. (This will give a sweetness but more importantly add colour.)

3   Bake for 45 minutes. Transfer the ingredients from the pan into a large saucepan and add the water, tomato purée, parsley and sage and bring to the boil; then turn down to a simmer and cook for 2½ hours or until you have approximately 2 pints (1.1 litres)of reduced stock. During this time skim off any scum which forms.

4   Strain the stock and leave to cool overnight. The next day skim off any fat which has risen to the top.

5   Peel the large potatoes and onion and grate coarsely. Mix together, season well and stir in the egg yolks.

6   Heat the olive oil in a large frying-pan and – using a large metal pastry-cutter as a mould – put the mould into the frying-pan and fill with a quarter of the mixture and press down to form the galette.

7   Do this four times, removing the mould each time. You will now have four galettes cooking in the pan. Sauté until golden brown and then turn over and cook the other side. These can be cooked beforehand and kept warm in the oven.

8   Trim the asparagus and peel the coarse ends. Poach for 5 minutes in boiling salted water whilst preparing the steak.

9   Pan-fry the steaks in a solid-based frying-pan coated with a little olive oil – the aim is to sear the meat and retain the juices. Cook to your liking.

10   Remove the steaks from the pan and then deglaze with the port; add 1 pint (600 ml) of stock and reduce rapidly by half. Pass through a sieve to remove any bits, then whisk in a good knob of butter which will slightly thicken the sauce and give it a shine.

11   To serve, take the 4 steaks and cut off any outer fat, then slice each steak at an angle into 6 or 8 slices. Place each cooked potato galette on to the centre of a hot dinner plate and arrange the slices of steak around it. Carefully spoon the sauce around the meat and then take 4 asparagus spears, cut them in half, and arrange in a crossed-swords formation in four positions around the plate.

BEEF COBBLER WITH WINTER SAVORY

Winter savory has always been one of the favourite herbs in Wales; together with rosemary, thyme and parsley, it holds a special place just outside the kitchen door. Hardy and peppery, it finds its way into many a hearty casserole. This cobbler, with its puffy golden scones on top and rich stew underneath, is a winner for the future.

SERVES 4

1½ lb (750 g) beef (stewing or shin)
8 oz (225 g) lamb's kidneys
seasoned plain flour
2 oz (50 g) good dripping or 2
tablespoons cooking oil (groundnut
or rapeseed)
2 onions, diced
2 leeks, washed and sliced
2 carrots, scrubbed and sliced
approx 1 pint (600 ml) beef stock

1 teaspoon winter savory
1 tablespoon tomato purée

For the scone topping:
3 oz (75 g) margarine or butter
8 oz (225 g) self-raising flour
salt
1 teaspoon winter savory
1 egg
milk to mix

1   Pre-heat the oven to gas mark 2, 300°F (150°C).

2   Cut the fat and sinew off the beef and kidneys and dice into 1 inch (2 cm) chunks. Toss in seasoned flour.

3   Heat the dripping or oil in a heavy-based casserole and fry the meat, a little at a time so that it browns on all sides. Remove from the pan and fry the onions, leeks and carrots until they colour.

4   Replace the meat and pour in enough beef stock to cover; add the herbs and tomato purée. Cover and cook gently for 2 hours.

5   Rub the margarine or butter into the flour; stir in the salt and herbs. Mix the beaten egg with a little milk and add to the flour to make a soft dough. Roll or pat out the dough on a floured surface. Cut into circles with a small cutter.

6   Remove the casserole from the oven and increase heat to gas mark 7, 425°F (220°C).

7   Place the scones on top of the meat, overlapping a little. Brush with milk, return to the hot oven and bake for 10–15 minutes until the crust is golden brown.

PUDDINGS

Natural 'tidy' housekeeping, blended with the Celtic sweet tooth, make the Welsh particular champions at puddings.

Oats, being a staple diet of the Welsh at one time, appeared in many sweet dishes. Oatcakes were crumbled into a dish of buttermilk to produce something of a modern-day muesli. In fact, Flummery, thought to be of Scottish descent, is very definitely Welsh, coming from the Welsh word Llymru.

A large creamy rice pudding was often baked on a shelf under the Sunday joint. Ken Goody, from the Cemlyn Restaurant in Harlech, can remember his mother's roast beef and also the riot that followed over scraping the rice pudding dish clean!

Country and townspeople alike were fond of collecting autumn berries, gathering windfalls, and even perhaps a little scrumping! This brought fruit into the kitchen to add the vital ingredients to many a pie or crumble.

Dairy produce has always held a strong place in rural Wales, with endless amounts of skimmed milk and buttermilk being available once the cream and butter had been removed for the market. This led to boiled milk puddings as well as buttermilk both for baking and as a refreshing and healthy drink. And no fruit tart would have been served without good thick cream!

Yoghurt, a recent arrival in Britain, is here to stay: it cooks well, is good for you and has earned its place on the Welsh table beside the cream jug. Being made 'on site', it is often served with honey for breakfast to lucky farmhouse guests.

Since the introduction of milk quotas at the beginning of the eighties dairy farmers have redirected their milk supplies into other dairy products and one of these is delicious dairy ice cream. These full-cream ices mixed with fresh fruit now compete for trade against the traditional ice cream parlours set up by a major influx of Italians during the last century. 'Sidoli' signs swing in the breeze beside 'Denbigh Farmhouse Ices'.

Baking comes naturally to the Welsh, and pastry made from locally milled flour and farm butter is short and light. This, combined with an abundance of wild hedgerow fruit, gives Welsh fruit slices and pies their favoured place in the hearts of local people.

WHINBERRY AND YOGHURT TART

Here is a recipe for a tart that makes the most of a few berries, be they whinberries (which you may know as bilberries, blaeberries or whortleberries), blackberries, redcurrants or blackcurrants. This pie has a touch of magic about it, for although it looks quite substantial it is really as light as a feather.

SERVES 4

8 oz (225 g) flour
pinch of salt
6 oz (175 g) butter
2 teaspoons caster sugar
1 medium egg yolk
1–2 tablespoons cold water
2 oz (50 g) whole brown almonds
1 lb (450 g) whinberries, blackberries, or
  blackcurrants, picked over

2 eggs, separated
¼ pint (150 ml) thick cream
¼ pint (150 ml) yoghurt
1 tablespoon lemon juice
4 oz (100 g) caster sugar
1 level tablespoon cornflour

1   Pre-heat the oven to gas mark 7, 425°F (220°C).

2   Sift the flour and salt into a large bowl; cut the butter into small lumps and drop into the flour. Using your fingertips, rub the butter into the flour until it resembles breadcrumbs. Add the sugar.

3   Mix the egg yolk with 1 tablespoon of water and stir into the mixture, adding the remaining water if the dough won't stick together. Chill the pastry for half an hour.

4   Pour boiling water over the almonds and leave for a couple of minutes before rinsing under the cold tap. Squeeze the almonds out of their brown skins, then chop or grind finely.

5   Pick over the fruit and discard any bruised berries.

6   On a floured surface, roll the pastry out into a large disc. Line a high-sided 8 inch (20 cm) loose-bottom flan tin with the pastry and scatter over the ground almonds and fruit. Bake in the oven for 15 minutes.

7   Separate the eggs and beat the cream, yoghurt, egg yolks, lemon juice and sugar together.

8   Whisk the egg whites until stiff and stir in the cornflour. Fold into the mixture and spread over the berries.

9 Turn the oven down to gas mark 5, 375°F (190°C) and bake the tart for 40–50 minutes, until well risen and golden brown.

PLUM PUDDING

This is just the kind of pudding you'll feel like after a day spent hiking over the Brecon Beacons. And if you happen to be staying in farmhouse accommodation, then you might be lucky. Nouvelle cuisine is not farmhouse style; you'll get big portions of the very best home cooking.

SERVES 4

2 oz (50 g) fresh white breadcrumbs
½ pint (300 ml) double cream
2 egg yolks
1 tablespoon white wine

¼ teaspoon cinnamon
1 heaped tablespoon caster sugar
12 Victoria plums
1 egg white

1 Pre-heat the oven to gas mark 4, 350°F (180°C).

2 Put the breadcrumbs in a bowl. Heat the cream in a saucepan until almost boiling. Pour over the crumbs and stir to blend. Cover the bowl and leave until cool; then stir in the egg yolks, wine, cinnamon and sugar.

3 Poach the fruit in a little water until barely tender, then drain. When cool enough to handle, skin the fruit, remove the stones and purée the flesh. Stir the purée into the cream and breadcrumb mixture.

4 Whisk the egg white until stiff and fold into the mixture. Pour into a lightly greased, shallow, ovenproof dish.

5 Bake in a moderate oven for about 40 minutes.

6 Serve hot with a bowl of lightly whipped cream or clotted cream, or try a frothy orange sauce (page 110).

CREAM HEARTS WITH FRESH STRAWBERRY SAUCE

*If I tell you that this dairy pudding is made from goat's and sheep's milk, will you
please promise to taste it before rejecting the whole idea!
Now that health shops sell freeze-dried goat's milk and vegetarian rennet, the
ingredients are easy to collect, and it really is fun to make your own curd cheese.
These hearts taste delicious and look pretty, and I'm sure this recipe will suit the
increasing number of people allergic to cow's milk.
The recipe takes 12 hours from start to finish, so either begin early in the morning or
prepare some of the processes the night before.
Cream hearts should be eaten very fresh.*

SERVES 4

18 fl oz (500 ml) goat's milk (1 packet
    dried)
1 teaspoon vegetarian rennet
1 pint (600 ml) Greek-style yoghurt
    (sheep's or cow's)
½ teaspoon grated lemon rind
1–2 tablespoons runny honey

For the berry sauce:
8 oz (225 g) fresh ripe strawberries,
    whinberries, raspberries or others
juice of ½ orange
honey to sweeten
grated nutmeg

1   Heat the milk to blood heat, stir in the rennet and leave for 10 minutes.

2   Line a metal sieve with muslin and pour the set milk into it. Leave to drain in a cool place for 2 hours, lifting the corners of the cloth from time to time to speed up the process.

3   Take the firm curd cheese and mix it with the yoghurt and lemon rind. Return it to the muslin-lined sieve and leave to drain again for a further 4 hours.

4   You should by now have a firm white cream. Press it through a sieve and then stir in the honey to taste.

5   Line 4 moulds, heart-shaped or ramekins, with clean muslin.

6   Divide the cream between the moulds and leave them for at least 6 hours or overnight to firm.

7 Stew the strawberries (or other fruit) in the smallest amount of water possible. Mash them through a very fine sieve; add the orange juice, honey to taste and a little grated nutmeg.

8 Spoon the pink sauce on to individual serving plates and turn out the cream hearts to sit on top.

Note: If you can't find any muslin then a clean J-cloth will improvise.

BAKED HONEY CUSTARD

This is an ideal way to use up a milk mountain and combine some really Welsh flavours.
It is traditional in Wales to decorate cawl or soup with marigold petals, and likewise milk puddings were often decorated with a scattering of rose or violet petals.

SERVES 4

1 pint (600 ml) milk
1 good tablespoon honey
1 dessertspoon caster sugar

4–5 eggs (depending on size)
nutmeg

1 Pre-heat the oven to gas mark 3, 325°F (160°C).

2 Warm the milk, honey and sugar and stir to blend.

3 Crack the eggs into a mixing bowl and gradually whisk them into the warm milk mixture. Strain into a 1½–2 pint (900 ml–1.2 litre) earthenware baking dish. Bake in the centre of the oven for 1–1½ hours or until the custard has set.

4 Sprinkle with a pinch of nutmeg and a scattering of rose or violet petals.

Note: I enjoy this honey custard with a little orange flower water or elderflower cordial added before baking.

SUMMER BERRY PUDDING

This is a wonderful pudding. Make it throughout the summer, with all the various summer fruits as they appear.
In June add some heads of elderflower to give it that mysterious flowery flavour; in the autumn add elderberries to increase the purple juices. When using a mixture of fruits I always stew the berries for a few minutes first before adding currants, so as to get the best flavour out of all the fruit without overcooking it.
The fatless sponge gives the summer pudding a better, lighter texture than bread.

SERVES 4

1½ lb (750 g) soft mixed fruit
(redcurrants, blackcurrants, cherries,
raspberries, loganberries, tayberries and
blackberries)
4 oz (100 g) caster sugar

For the sponge cake:
2 eggs, separated
4 oz (100 g) caster sugar
3 oz (75 g) plain flour

1   Pre-heat the oven to gas mark 4, 350°F (180°C).

2   In a large bowl, whisk the egg whites until meringue-like. Continue to whisk as you add the egg yolks and sugar a little at a time, until you have a pale yellow mousse.

3   Fold in the sifted flour and turn the mixture into an oiled 8 inch (20 cm) tin.

4   Bake in the oven for about 20 minutes.

5   Pick over the fruit and remove any stalks. Stew the fruit gently with a minimum of liquid until soft, starting with the berries, then adding the currants a few minutes later. Finally add the sugar (and 3 heads of elderflower if available) and leave the fruit to cool.

6   Line a 2 pint (1.2 litre) bowl with ½ inch (1 cm) slices of the sponge. Spoon in half the fruit with its juice. Cover with another layer of sponge and fill to the top with the remainder of the fruit. Cover again with slices of sponge.

7   Fit a saucer inside the top rim of the bowl and place a weight of about 2 lb (1 kg) on top. Leave in a cool place overnight.

8   Invert the bowl on to a serving dish and serve the summer pudding with pouring cream.

PEARS IN A SPICED SPONGE

Mead-making has long been a Welsh hobby and although it is no longer made commercially there are still a remarkable amount of keen amateur apiarists who brew it. Metheglin, a mead-based drink flavoured with rosemary, thyme and bay leaves, was a great favourite with Queen Elizabeth I and she used the recipe from her ancestral Tudor home at Penmynydd in Anglesey.
If you can't find any mead, use a combination of white wine and honey.

SERVES 4

3 ripe (but not soft) pears	4 oz (100 g) butter
1 cinnamon stick	4 oz (100 g) soft brown sugar
4 cloves	2 eggs, beaten
½ pint (300 ml) mead or dry white wine	6 oz (175 g) self-raising flour
1 tablespoon honey	1 teaspoon powdered ginger

1 Pre-heat the oven to gas mark 4, 350°F (180°C).

2 Peel and core the pears; halve them and place in a layer in the base of a large saucepan. Add the cinnamon stick and cloves and cover with mead or wine and honey.

3 Bring the pan to the boil and simmer or poach very gently until the pears are soft but not mushy. (This can be done very successfully in a microwave oven.)

4 Remove the pears with a slotted spoon or fish slice and arrange in the bottom of a heatproof casserole or cake tin. Spoon over 2 tablespoons of the syrup.

5 Cream together the butter and sugar until pale and fluffy; add the beaten egg a little at a time, beating well after each addition. Fold in the flour and ginger, adding some of the spare syrup to give a dropping consistency.

6 Spread the mixture on top of the pears. Bake for about 45 minutes until the top is crisp and golden brown.

7 Turn out on to a dish and serve with whipped cream to which some of the remaining syrup has been added.

WELSH RICE PUDDING

Rice pudding must conjure up memories for everyone: they may be of loathing left over from schooldays or of pure pleasure in recalling that sweet, comforting smell synonymous with Sunday lunch.

In Wales the tradition was to serve rice pudding after a roast; baking the pudding underneath the meat made good use of the lit oven and provided the family with a favourite treat.

If your rice pudding reflections are not happy, then I beg you to try this recipe of Ken Goody's, from the Cemlyn Restaurant in Harlech. It may convert you to the noble grain for ever.

MAKES 5 GOOD PORTIONS

½ pint (300 ml) milk
½ pint (300 ml) single cream
½ vanilla pod
2 oz (50 g) round pudding rice
1 oz (25 g) caster sugar
2 oz (50 g) unsalted butter

2 whole eggs
2 egg yolks
2 tablespoons whisky
4 oz (100 g) dark, coarse-cut marmalade
1 oz (25 g) demerara sugar (optional)
(for brulée) 2 oz (50 g) caster sugar

1   Pre-heat the oven to gas mark 4, 350°F (180°C).

2   In a saucepan, bring the milk, cream and vanilla pod to the boil; add the rice, stir and then simmer gently for 20 minutes until the rice is tender. Stir in the sugar. Remove the vanilla pod, which may be dried and used again.

3   Using some of the butter, grease a 2 pint (1.2 litre) bowl or pie dish.

4   Beat the 2 whole eggs and 2 yolks with the whisky and marmalade and stir into the rice mixture. Pour into the dish and dot the top with the remaining butter (and a little demerara sugar if you are serving the rice pudding hot).

5   Bake for 30 minutes.

6   Either serve the rice pudding hot, straight from the oven, or leave to cool and serve as a Rice Brulée.

Rice Brulée:
Pre-heat the grill to its hottest; dust the cool rice pudding with caster sugar and grill until a crisp caramel forms on top. Chill before serving.

BLACKBERRY BREAD PUDDING

*This is a wonderful autumn pudding: bread soaked in blackberry juice served with a
jug of pouring cream. If you can find traditional crusty-baked bread rather than
modern steam-baked, so much the better, for it will absorb more of the blackberry
juices and give the pudding a softer texture.*
*Frances Roughley, of the Gelli Fawr Country House at Pontfaen, near Newport,
Pembrokeshire, makes individual ones, lining little ramekin dishes with bread. She
says that her guests really enjoy cutting into their very own blackberry bread
pudding.*

SERVES 4

*8–10 slices thin, day-old bread, crusts cut
    off*
juice of 1 orange
2–3 tablespoons water

4–6 oz (100–150 g) caster sugar
1½ lb (750 g) blackberries
1 tablespoon blackcurrant cassis liqueur

1 Rinse a 1½ pint (900 ml) pudding basin with cold water. Cut a
circle of bread to fit the bottom of the basin and some wedge-shaped
pieces to fit around the sides; press bread firmly to line the basin so
that there are no gaps. Keep a few slices of bread to cover the top.

2 In a small saucepan, heat the orange juice, water and sugar; stir to
dissolve. Add the blackberries and cook for a few minutes. Take off the
heat and strain off about ¼ pint (150 ml) of the fruit juices into a jug
and keep.

3 Pour the fruit and remaining juices into the bread-lined bowl.
Arrange the remaining bread over the fruit and cover with a saucer that
fits snugly into the top of the bowl. Place a weight (I use a large tin of
baked beans) on top of the saucer and leave overnight.

4 Next day turn the blackberry pudding out on to a large serving
dish. Add the cassis to the reserved blackberry juices in the jug and
pour over.

5 Serve with lashings of thick pouring cream.

LAVENDER SYLLABUB

The earliest syllabubs were made by taking the milk still warm from the cow and mixing it with ale or cider. This was allowed to stand until a curd formed on top of the whey, which posed a practical problem – the dish had to be partly eaten, partly drunk. Later on, wine was used in place of ale, and cream instead of milk.
By the eighteenth century, the proportion of cream was increased and the wine reduced until the final mixture was uniformly thick and of a delicious lightness and delicacy of flavour.

SERVES 4

4 fl oz (120 ml) water
4 large heads of lavender or 1 tablespoon
   dried lavender
4 oz (100 g) caster sugar

juice of ½ lemon
12 fl oz (355 ml) double cream
3 tablespoons dry white wine

1   Boil the water and pour on to the lavender; leave to infuse for 20 minutes.

2   Strain the lavender water and pour into a small saucepan; add the sugar and bring the syrup to the boil. Continue boiling for 1 minute. Cool the syrup, pour into a deep bowl, then add the lemon juice and wine.

3   Using a hand or rotary whisk, slowly add the cream to the wine mixture; continue to whisk hard until the mixture thickens to a soft peak.

4   Spoon into glasses and stand in a cool place until needed. (Choose a cool larder in preference to a fridge.)

5   Serve with plain crisp biscuits.

This syllabub will keep for 2 to 3 days, although the cream and wine may begin to separate.

RHUBARB AND NUT CRUMBLE

In today's sophisticated world we can buy almost anything at any time of the year. What a pity! With the arrival of each season there are no special flavours to look forward to; no tradition of soft summer fruits, autumn berries or winter root vegetables. I can remember a time when rhubarb crumble meant spring had arrived. The sharpness of rhubarb combines well with the hearty crumble topping, and I find that the orange and ginger flavours blend well. Choose the fruit young and pink, cut off both ends and remove any tough strings from the length. Avoid cooking rhubarb in aluminium since the acid in the fruit reacts with the metal. Use glass or stainless steel if possible.

SERVES 4

1 lb (450 g) rhubarb
grated rind and juice of 1 orange
1 teaspoon grated fresh ginger
2 oz (50 g) caster sugar
4 oz (100 g) self-raising wholemeal flour
pinch of salt

2 oz (50 g) butter or polyunsaturated
  margarine
2 oz (50 g) demerara sugar
1 teaspoon mixed spice
2 oz (50 g) mixed nuts, walnuts, almonds
  or hazelnuts

1 Pre-heat the oven to gas mark 4, 350°F (180°C).

2 Cut the rhubarb into 1 inch (2.5 cm) sticks and put in the bottom of a 2 pint (1.2 litre) pie dish. Add the grated rind and juice of the orange, the ginger and caster sugar.

3 In a large bowl, mix the flour and salt and, using your fingertips, rub in the butter until the mixture looks like breadcrumbs. Stir in the demerara sugar, spice and nuts.

4 Spoon the crumble mixture over the rhubarb and cook for 30 minutes until crisp and golden.

5 Serve with Baked Honey Custard (see p. 103).

WELSH APPLE PUDDING WITH FROTHY ORANGE SAUCE

The perfect pudding for a cold autumn's day especially when there's a glut of cooking apples. You probably have the other simple ingredients in the larder to make this warming pudding. The batter topping rises up like a soufflé and looks spectacular as it crisps to a golden brown. It is light as a feather though and, together with the frothy orange sauce, the pudding will vanish in moments.

SERVES 4

1 lb (450 g) cooking apples, peeled, cored and sliced
4 tablespoons water
1 tablespoon honey
4 cloves
1½ oz (40 g) butter
2 oz (50 g) plain flour
¾ pint (450 ml) milk
2 oz (50 g) caster sugar

2 eggs, separated
1 teaspoon grated orange rind

For the sauce:
2 egg yolks (size 2–3)
2 oz (50 g) soft brown sugar
3 tablespoons freshly squeezed orange juice

1   Pre-heat the oven to gas mark 5, 375°F (190°C).

2   Stew the apples in the water with the honey and cloves until tender. Take out the cloves and put the apples in a well-buttered ovenproof dish.

3   In a small saucepan, melt the butter, stir in the flour and then the milk. Bring to the boil, stirring constantly. Cool slightly.

4   Add the sugar, egg yolks and orange rind.

5   Whisk the egg whites till stiff and fold into the batter. Pour over the apples and bake for 45–50 minutes.

6   For the sauce, whisk the egg yolks and sugar together until thick and creamy-pale. Put the bowl over a pan of gently simmering water, whisk in the orange juice and continue whisking until the sauce bulks up into a froth.

7   Serve immediately with the hot apple pudding.

ELDERFLOWER CHAMPAGNE, JELLY AND SORBET

Similar to elderflower cordial, this recipe of Margaret Rees for elderflower champagne from the Cobblers Restaurant in Llandybie can be used for a variety of recipes. Although the recipe recommends that the champagne be used within two weeks, Margaret has had few explosions from her cellars!

Elderflower champagne:
3 heads of elderflower
1 tablespoon white wine vinegar

8 pints (4.8 litres) water
1½ lb (750 g) granulated sugar
1 lemon

Combine all the ingredients in a sterilised container and leave to stand in a cool place for 48 hours. Strain and pour into screw-top bottles. (It will make about 1 gallon.)

Elderflower champagne jelly:
1 oz (25 g) gelatine

3 tablespoons water
1¾ pints (1 litre) elderflower champagne

1 Dissolve the gelatine in 2 tablespoons of cold water, and 1 tablespoon of boiling water; place over a pan of warm water until all the grains have disappeared.

2 Pour the champagne into a large bowl and add the melted gelatine. Stir and pour into a serving dish to set in a fridge.

Fresh fruits can be set in the jelly, e.g. melon, orange slices, kiwi fruits, sliced peaches, sliced nectarines, strawberries etc.

Elderflower sorbet:
1¾ pints (1 litre) elderflower champagne
2 egg whites

1 Place the elderflower champagne in a container in the freezer until it has lightly frozen. Remove and whisk or use the food processor to break the ice into a mush.

2 Repeat this process twice, then fold in 2 whisked egg whites and blend until the mixture resembles snow.

HONEY AND LEMON YOGHURT ICE CREAM

In Wales, Rachael's Dairy at Towyn provides us with organic natural yoghurt made from the milk of their pedigree Guernsey herd, so our yoghurt is a lovely rich golden colour and quite pure. They make excellent cream, too. Perhaps, as they make such vital ingredients for this ice cream, I had better give them my recipe!

SERVES 4

1 lb (450 g) natural yoghurt
2 tablespoons runny honey
2 oz (50 g) caster sugar

the juice of 2 lemons and the grated rind of 1
¼ pint (150 ml) double cream

1 Mix the yoghurt, honey, sugar, lemon juice and rind and cream together and pour into a freezable container.

2 Freeze for 2 hours, then beat the ice cream hard to break up any icy particles that may have formed.

3 Return the ice cream to the freezer and freeze until needed.

4 Serve in scoops from a pretty glass bowl, decorated with slices of fresh lemon.

MINT SORBET

Fresh and minty, this is a really refreshing sorbet. Mint is grown in most gardens in Wales; after all, who would serve roast lamb without it?
The art of making a good sorbet is to remember to let it soften a little out of the freezer before serving it, so pop it into the fridge for 20 minutes before you want to eat it.

SERVES 4

6 large sprigs mint, any variety
3 oz (75 g) caster sugar
½ pint (300 ml) water

juice of 1 large lemon
1 egg white
4 tiny sprigs mint to decorate

1 Wash the mint and shake it dry.

2 Put the sugar and water in a pan and boil until the sugar has dissolved. Drop in the mint, cover the pan and turn off the heat. Leave for 20 minutes to infuse, then taste. If the flavour is weak, bring the liquid to the boil again, cover the pan, turn off the heat and leave for a further 10 minutes.

3   When the flavour is strong enough, strain the liquid into a rigid container, add the lemon juice and leave to cool. Freeze for about an hour until the sorbet is half frozen.

4   Beat the egg white in a bowl until it is stiff. Fold it into the sorbet and return it to the freezer until frozen to a firm mush (about 1 hour).

5   To serve, spoon into 4 glasses and decorate each one with a tiny sprig of mint.

FLUMMERY OR LLYMRU

Flummery, or Llymru as the Welsh first called it, was a traditional Celtic dish. Fine oatmeal was steeped in water for several hours, the liquid strained off and boiled until it turned into a brown blancmange.
Today, health and fashion dictate that we should eat more roughage in the way of cereals and it seems wrong to savour the oat-soaked juices rather than the actual oatmeal, so I have adapted my recipe to make a twentieth-century flummery.
The Scots might add their whisky, but I prefer Flummery served with honey and fresh fruit, the perfect summer porridge.

SERVES 4

4 oz (100 g) medium oatmeal
2 tablespoons heather honey
1 tablespoon fresh lemon juice
8 oz (225 g) fresh fruit, blackberries,
   chopped apple, banana, strawberries etc

¼ pint (150 ml) buttermilk, fromage frais
   or double cream

1   Soak the oatmeal in cold water overnight.

2   Next day strain off any excess water and stir in the honey, lemon juice and fresh fruit. Softly whisk the cream and fold gently into the oatmeal mixture.

3   Serve the flummery at breakfast or as a pudding. It makes a delicious, healthy, filling snack.

BAKING

In the TV programme on baking we see, in the space of half an hour, the demise of the real loaf! The majority of our pre-packed bread is full of additives (not harmful ones); it lasts for weeks, and is inexpensive. We visit one of the most modern bakeries in Wales where as many as 25,000 rolls are produced an hour. We see rolls moving on conveyers in and out of steam rooms, ovens, cooling racks and finally into 'gas-packed' cartons.

Then we cool the pace and spend a little time learning how it takes five hours to produce just one or two honest, old-fashioned loaves. Using organic flours, natural yeast, oil and water, the dough is kneaded by hand and baked in brick ovens.

So we're led to believe that traditional bread takes too long to prepare, would occupy too many bakers and cost too much. Well, you can't have your cake and eat it.

Or can you? Many do! Traditional bread is selling like hot cakes from the bakery at St Fagan's Folk Museum, where customers queue all day and the baker, Chris Aston, simply can't make enough.

And there are other real bakeries in Wales. As many as nine water mills have recently been restored to working order and grain is again being ground traditionally by stone. These mills bake with their own flour and produce a very different bread than you will find neatly sliced in any polythene wrapper.

The Welsh are traditionally fine bakers, and they have talent with the griddle too. The dextrous housewife could bake a loaf of bread and a variety of scones and small cakes on her flat bakestone. Welsh cakes, moist scones containing currants, are still griddled by a large part of the population in Wales; and how the Welsh love their *crempog* or pancakes.

Eleri Davies at Pentre Farmhouse, Lampeter, Dyfed, still uses her bakestone to make individual fruit turnovers, in very much the same manner as her grandmother did. But a non-stick bakestone now replaces the solid iron one: it heats in a quarter of the time and gives an even heat. Eleri makes a variety of fillings such as rhubarb and raspberry, apple and cinnamon or gooseberry and elderflower. She serves the sugar-coated 'tarten planc' with a fruit sauce and a bowl of cream.

BARABRITH

Barabrith literally means speckled bread; speckled with a handful of dried fruit that would be added to the last lump of dough at the end of a day's baking to make a rich tea bread.
There are many recipes for Barabrith using self-raising flour which turn out more like a cake, but I think it should be made from a basic yeast dough. I do cheat, though, by using easy-bake yeast!

MAKES 3 LB (1.5 KG) DOUGH

1 lb (450 g) mixed dried fruit
7 fl oz (200 ml) cold tea
12 oz (350 g) stoneground wholemeal flour
12 oz (350 g) strong white flour
2 sachets easy-bake yeast

1½ teaspoons mixed spice
6 oz (175 g) soft brown sugar
4 oz (100 g) butter, melted
2 eggs, beaten
½ teaspoon salt
honey

1   Soak the fruit for 3 hours in the cold tea (longer will soften the fruit so much that it breaks up in the mixer).

2   Brush 3 × 1 lb (450 g) tins or equivalent with oil and line the bottom with greaseproof paper.

3   Put the flour into a large warm bowl and stir in the yeast, spice and sugar. Melt the butter and pour it into the flour together with the eggs and salt. Add the fruit and cold tea and knead gently for about 5 minutes or until the dough is smooth and elastic.

4   Using a spatula, spread the dough to fit into the baking tins and leave to prove in a warm place for at least 2 hours. (Rising may take a long time due to the richness of the dough.)

5   Pre-heat the oven to gas mark 6, 400°F (200°C).

6   Bake the Barabrith on the shelf below the centre of the oven for 15 minutes; turn the heat down to gas mark 3, 325°F (160°C) for a further 45–60 minutes, covering the top of the loaf tins with foil if it browns too much on top.

7   Brush the cooked Barabrith with warm honey to glaze. Serve sliced and buttered.

Barabrith should be wrapped in foil and stored before use if possible – to improve the texture and flavour.

SPICED HONEY LOAF

I'd like to be able to say that this loaf improves with keeping, but alas, mine never even gets as far as the cake tin. However, it only takes seconds to prepare!

MAKES 1 LOAF

¼ pint (150 ml) boiling water
4 level tablespoons runny honey
8 oz (225 g) plain flour
pinch of salt

4 oz (100 g) caster sugar
2 teaspoons mixed spice
1 level teaspoon baking powder
1 level teaspoon bicarbonate of soda

1 Pre-heat the oven to gas mark 3, 325°F (160°C).

2 Boil the water and stir in the honey. Oil and flour a 2 lb (1 kg) loaf tin.

3 Sieve the flour with the salt and add the sugar and spice. Using a wooden spoon, add the melted honey and water, beating until bubbles appear. Stir in the baking powder and bicarbonate of soda.

4 Pour the mixture into the bread tin and bake for about 45 minutes or until a skewer inserted into the loaf comes out clean.

5 Serve the loaf warm or cold, spread with butter or cream cheese.

TEISEN LAP

This simple fruit cake is typical of an everyday cake made by many Welsh housewives. Teisen is Welsh for cake and Lap means moist, so this is just the sort of cake that would have travelled well down the pit in a miner's lunchbox.

8 oz (225 g) plain flour
1 level teaspoon baking powder
½ teaspoon ground nutmeg
4 oz (100 g) butter
1 oz (25 g) lard

4 oz (100 g) caster sugar
4 oz (100 g) currants
2 eggs
2 tablespoons milk

1 Pre-heat the oven to gas mark 4, 350°F (180°C).

2 Sieve the flour, baking powder and nutmeg into a bowl. Rub in the butter and lard with your fingers. Stir in the caster sugar and currants.

3   Beat the eggs and add to the dry ingredients. Mix thoroughly and add the milk to give a soft consistency.

4   Spread the mixture into a greased and floured 8 inch (20 cm) sandwich tin or tart plate.

5   Bake for 20 minutes in the pre-set oven, then turn down to gas mark 3, 325°F (160°C) for a further 35 minutes.

6   Dust with caster sugar before serving.

MRS PEEL'S BLACKCURRANT BUNS

This recipe was given to me by a friend, Fiona Peel, who has a fruit farm in Castleton in Gwent. She uses the fruits as they come into season and turns them into jams, jellies, chutneys, pies, buns and ice creams which she sells from the farm shop and in her tea shop.

MAKES 15 BUNS

5 oz (150 g) plain flour
3 oz (75 g) caster sugar
3 teaspoons baking powder
1 egg
3 fl oz (85 ml) milk
3 oz (75 g) soft vegetarian margarine
(e.g. sunflower)

3 oz (75 g) blackcurrants, topped and tailed

For the topping:
1 oz (25 g) caster sugar
1 teaspoon ground cinnamon

1   Pre-heat the oven to gas mark 4, 350°F (180°C).

2   Grease and flour 15 deep bun tins.

3   In a large bowl or food processor, mix the flour, sugar and baking powder. Combine the egg with the milk and add to the dry ingredients with the soft margarine. Beat or process until smooth. Fold in the blackcurrants by hand.

4   Spoon the mixture into the prepared bun tins, filling only three-quarters full.

5   Mix the caster sugar and cinnamon and sprinkle over the top of the buns. Bake for 20 minutes.

ELERI'S TARTEN PLANC

It is surprising just how many Welsh homes still harbour a bakestone or planc for cooking oatcakes, pancakes and griddle breads. Some are old, well used and heavy, whilst others are new, non-stick, very light and electric.
Eleri Davies has both kinds, for in her busy lifestyle as a farmer's wife who runs a guesthouse she needs to be able to provide a great deal of food very fast for her hungry guests.
This sugar-glistening, crisp, crusty fruit pie recipe of Eleri's is more than tempting. If you feel daunted at the thought of turning a large pie over on your griddle or frying-pan, then she suggests that you should start by making some small pies, and graduate on to a family tarten planc.
Eleri suggests a range of tangy fruit combinations for the filling, but almost any fruit is suitable, so adapt the recipe to suit yourself. Make your tarts very smart by serving them with a fruit sauce poured carefully round the edge of the plate.

SERVES 4

For the shortcrust pastry:
3 oz (75 g) margarine or butter
3 oz (75 g) lard
12 oz (350 g) plain white or a mixture of white and wholemeal flour
cold water
caster sugar for dredging over baked cakes
(cinnamon can be added too)

Suggested sweetened fruit purée fillings:
gooseberries with elderflower champagne

rhubarb and ginger
rhubarb and raspberries
apple and grated orange rind
apple and sultanas or raisins with brown sugar and cinnamon
apple and blackberries
blackcurrants and lemon juice

For the fruit sauce:
fresh fruit to stew
sugar
liqueur or wine for extra flavour

1 Stew the fruit in a minimum of water; add sugar to taste. Pulp or purée the fruit and leave to cool.

2 Make the sauce in the same way but slacken the fruit purée to a pouring consistency by adding a little liqueur or sweet wine.

3 Rub the fats into the flour until the mixture looks like fine breadcrumbs. Add enough cold water to make a firm but not damp dough. Leave to rest for 30 minutes before rolling out fairly thinly on a floured board.

4 Cut the dough into rounds, using a 6 or 8 inch (15–20 cm) plate as a guide, or make little tarts with a 3 inch (7.5 cm) cutter. Dampen the edges of the rounds with cold water.

5   Place sweetened fruit purée on a pastry disc and cover.

6   Bake on a greased, heated planc or heavy frying-pan for 2–3 minutes each side, turning carefully.

7   Sprinkle over caster sugar and serve hot or cold with fruit sauce.

BAKESTONE BREAD

In the past when butter was churned in all Welsh dairy farms the residue buttermilk was put to very good use by the farmer's wife. Its use in baking was widespread. Buttermilk gives the dough for this bakestone or soda bread an excellent lightness and delicious flavour. Imagine cooking it on the bakestone or griddle – it takes an experienced baker to get the loaf to rise without burning the top or the bottom. I suggest that you cook your Bakestone Bread in the oven, but for the purist, please do attempt to cook your loaf on a griddle or even in a frying-pan!

MAKES 1 LOAF

1 lb (450 g) plain flour
2 level teaspoons bicarbonate of soda
2 level teaspoons cream of tartar
1 level teaspoon salt
1 oz (25 g) butter or lard

1–2 level teaspoons caster sugar (optional)
9 fl oz (275 ml) buttermilk mixed with 1 fl oz (25 ml) fresh milk, or ½ pint (300 ml) milk soured with lemon juice

1   Pre-heat the oven to gas mark 6, 400°F (200°C).

2   Sift the flour, bicarbonate of soda, cream of tartar and salt into a bowl. Cut up the butter or lard and rub it into the flour with your fingers until the mixture resembles fine breadcrumbs. Add the sugar.

3   Make a well in the centre of the flour, add the buttermilk or soured milk and mix to a soft but manageable dough, working the ingredients with a round-bladed knife. Add more milk if necessary.

4   Quickly turn the dough on to a floured surface, knead it lightly, shape into a 7 inch (18 cm) round and flatten it slightly.

5   Mark the round into four with the back of a knife, set it on a floured baking tray and bake in the centre of the oven for about 30 minutes.

6   Cool on a wire rack and serve fresh.

BABS WEBB'S CUT AND COME AGAIN FRUIT CAKE

The smell of freshly baked fruit cake permeating Babs' and Bill's cottage on baking day is mouth-watering, and Babs is justly famous for it.

8 oz (225 g) plain flour
pinch of salt
4 oz (100 g) margarine or butter
4 oz (100 g) brown sugar
12 oz (350 g) mixed dried fruit

2 eggs, beaten
1 dessertspoon vinegar
1 tablespoon cider or beer
1 tablespoon marmalade or jam
a little cold milk

1 Pre-heat the oven to gas mark 4, 350°F (180°C).

2 Sift the flour with the salt into a large bowl. Cut the margarine or butter into small dice and toss into the flour. Using fingertips, rub the fat into the flour until it looks like fine breadcrumbs.

3 Stir in the sugar and mixed fruit. Pour in the beaten eggs, vinegar, cider and marmalade or jam. Stir to blend and add a little cold milk if necessary to make a soft dropping consistency.

4 Spread into a buttered 2 pint (1.2 litre) baking tin and bake in the centre of the oven for about an hour.

OATCAKES

Welsh oatcakes are similar to Scottish oatcakes but thinner. Both have ancient Celtic origins and are traditionally cooked on a bakestone in Wales. There is a certain art to mixing, rolling or 'rounding', and baking oatcakes, the aim being to achieve an oatcake the size of a dinner plate and as thin as possible.
Being a beginner to the art, I must admit to cheating a little. My oatcakes are made infinitely easier to handle by mixing the oatmeal with an equal quantity of wholewheat flour and binding the mixture with a higher proportion of fat.

MAKES ENOUGH FOR 4

6 oz (175 g) medium oatmeal
6 oz (175 g) wholewheat flour
1 teaspoon salt

¼ teaspoon bicarbonate of soda
3 oz (75 g) margarine, butter or bacon fat
about 2 tablespoons cold water

1 Pre-heat the oven to gas mark 3, 325°F (160°C) or oil and heat your bakestone.

2   In a large bowl mix the oatmeal, flour, salt and bicarbonate of soda. Rub in the fat, using your fingertips.

3   Mix to a soft but not sticky dough with the cold water.

4   On a board dusted with wholewheat flour roll out to a large circle about 10 inches (25 cm) in diameter using only half the dough. Either cut the dough into circles using a pastry cutter or leave as one large disc, dividing into 8 portions, like a shortbread.

5   Bake in the pre-set oven for about 20 minutes until pale gold, or griddle, turning once after a few minutes in order to brown both sides.

A STACK OF PANCAKES

Traditionally baked as a birthday celebration treat, this recipe is naughty from beginning to end, but because it's pancakes it goes down well in Wales!

MAKES ENOUGH FOR 4

4 oz (100 g) self-raising flour
pinch of salt
1 oz (25 g) caster sugar
1 whole egg

1 egg yolk
¼ pint (150 ml) milk
2 oz (50 g) melted butter
1 oz (25 g) currants

1   Sift the flour into a large bowl and add the salt and sugar.

2   Mix the egg and extra yolk with the milk and melted butter and stir this into the dry ingredients, beating well until you have a smooth batter. Fold in the currants. (Alternatively, put the eggs, milk and melted butter into a liquidiser and then add the dry ingredients. Whisk till smooth and add the currants.)

3   Heat a griddle or large heavy-based frying-pan and rub a piece of oiled paper over the surface. Spread two tablespoons of batter over the surface of the pan to make a large disc. When bubbles appear, turn the pancake over to cook the other side; the mixture should make 4.

4   To serve, spread each pancake with butter and sprinkle with caster sugar and a little grated nutmeg. Stack the pancakes on top of each other in a pile. Serve warm.

WELSH CAKES

As soon as you stop for a cup of tea on entering the Principality, a sugar-covered, currant-filled, spicy Welsh Cake will warm your heart towards the Welsh. This is Meudwen Stephens' recipe for Welsh Cakes which, with the aid of her mother, she prepares in enormous quantities. Meudwen says the secret of making Welsh Cakes is to cook them briskly on both sides so that they stay moist in the middle. Take care not to burn them though!
In Wales they are baked on a heavy iron bakestone. Failing this, use a heavy-based frying-pan or casserole.

MAKES ENOUGH FOR 4

8 oz (25 g) self-raising flour
pinch of salt
1 teaspoon mixed spice
2 oz (50 g) butter or margarine
2 oz (50 g) lard

3 oz (75 g) caster sugar
3 oz (75 g) currants and sultanas, mixed
1 egg, beaten
1 teaspoon golden syrup

1 Sieve the flour, salt and spice into a mixing bowl. Rub in the fats until the mixture looks like fine breadcrumbs. Add the sugar and dried fruit.

2 Pour in the beaten egg and syrup and stir to make a fairly firm dough.

3 On a floured board, roll or press the dough out to approximately ¼ inch (5 mm) thick. Cut into rounds with a 1½ inch (4 cm) or 2 inch (5 cm) cutter.

4 Bake the Welsh Cakes on a medium hot griddle, turning once, until golden brown on both sides but still a little soft in the middle.

5 Dust the Welsh Cakes liberally with caster sugar whilst still hot. They are best eaten straight from the griddle, but will keep for up to 10 days in an airtight container.

WELSH TEACAKES

Brought up in Pembrokeshire, my neighbour Ruth Robertson remembers when there was fresh bread every day and always cakes for tea! Should an unexpected guest arrive, then teacakes would be rustled up immediately, and served hot from the oven, spread liberally with farm butter and home-made jam.
It is not surprising that most traditional Welsh cookery books have two chapters, one for baking and the other for everything else!

MAKES ENOUGH FOR 4

7 oz (200 g) plain flour
1½ teaspoons baking powder
pinch of salt
3 oz (75 g) butter
2 oz (50 g) caster sugar

1 egg
3 tablespoons milk
6 oz (175 g) mixed dried fruit including
  cut mixed peel
beaten egg white
granulated sugar

1 Pre-heat the oven to gas mark 5, 375°F (190°C).

2 Sieve the flour with the baking powder and salt.

3 Cream the butter and sugar till light and fluffy; add the egg, beating hard. Stir in the milk and mixed dried fruit and fold in the flour. Leave in a cool place for 10 minutes.

4 Form the dough into small balls about the size of a squash ball. Brush the tops with lightly beaten egg white, then sprinkle over granulated sugar.

5 Place the teacakes 2 inches (5 cm) apart, sugar side up, on a greased tray and bake for 15 minutes until brown.

6 Serve the teacakes warm, split in half and buttered.

TINKER'S CAKES

These tasty little cakes date back to when tinkers travelled through Wales mending pots and pans, I imagine that a tempting plate of fresh cakes could persuade them to become regular visitors!
The grated apple in these griddle cakes gives them a pleasant soft texture and the cinnamon adds a touch of spice. If you don't have a griddle, use a heavy-based frying-pan. Prepare it for griddling by rubbing a piece of oiled kitchen paper over the surface before heating.

MAKES 10–12

8 oz (225 g) flour
pinch of salt
4 oz (100 g) butter
½ teaspoon ground cinnamon

3 oz (75 g) soft brown sugar
1 medium-sized cooking apple
1 egg yolk
1 tablespoon milk

1 Sieve the flour into a large bowl, add the salt and with the tips of your fingers rub the butter into the flour until it looks like fine breadcrumbs. Add the sugar and cinnamon.

2 Peel the apple, then grate it straight into the flour mixture, stirring to stop any brown colour forming.

3 Mix the egg yolk with the milk and stir into the mixture to make a firm dough. Press together with your hands and turn on to a floured board.

4 Roll or pat out to about ¼ inch (5 mm) thick. Shape into small discs with a pastry cutter.

5 Heat the griddle over a medium heat. Cook the Tinker's Cakes gently on one side for about 3 minutes, then turn over to griddle the other.

6 Serve the Tinker's Cakes warm from the griddle, sprinkled with caster sugar.

ABERFFRAW CAKES

These rich shortbread biscuits are said to come from the small seaside village of Aberffraw on the south coast of Anglesey. They take their shape from the scallop shells which were traditionally used to mould them; not large scallops, but the special smaller queen scallops from Cardigan Bay on the west coast. Let the children have a hand in preparing the shortbread, pressing the mixture into the shells to make the pretty shape.

MAKES ENOUGH FOR **4**

8 oz (225 g) flour	*3 oz (75 g) caster sugar*
pinch of salt	*1 teaspoon mixed spice*
5 oz (150 g) butter	*1 egg yolk*

1 Pre-heat the oven to gas mark 5, 375°F (190°C).

2 Sift the flour and salt into a large mixing bowl. With cool hands rub the butter into the flour until it resembles fine breadcrumbs. Lift your hands high out of the bowl while you are doing this so that the butter doesn't melt and make the mixture sticky.

3 Stir in the sugar and spice, then the egg yolk, with the back of a knife blade until the mixture begins to stick together, and then press gently with your hands. The heat of your hands will make the mixture stick together, and as soon as it is a dough leave it in a cool place for 10 minutes. (The whole of this process can, of course, be done in seconds in a food processor.)

4 Press a small amount of the shortbread dough into a small scallop shell and tap out on to the table. (Alternatively roll or press the dough out on to a floured board and use a pastry cutter to make shortbread biscuits.)

5 Bake the Aberffraw biscuits on a greased baking sheet for about 10 minutes until golden but not brown. Leave on the tray for a few minutes before moving to a cooling tray.

HUNDRED PER CENT WHOLEMEAL BREAD

After my visit to the traditional Y-Felin corn mill at St Dogmael's near Cardigan in Dyfed I felt inspired to bake some bread using the flour I had bought.
Michael and Jane Hall are founder members of the Traditional Corn Millers' Guild. Members are all wind- and water-millers, who run their mills using primarily natural power to produce stone-ground meals and flours. Stone-grinding produces a nutty-flavoured meal with the wheat oil being gently released by the warm but not hot friction generated between the stones.
Making good bread depends very much on the quality of the flour. Wholemeal flour (or wholewheat flour) is so called because the whole of the wheat grain is in it; nothing is added – by law – and nothing taken away.

MAKES 2 LOAVES

3 lb (1.5 kg) 100% wholemeal flour
1 dessertspoon salt
2 oz (50 g) fresh yeast or equivalent dried
granules (but not easy-bake yeast)
1 dessertspoon brown sugar
1¾ pints (1 litre) water

1 Pre-heat the oven to gas mark 8, 450°F (230°C).

2 Oil and flour 2 × 2 lb (1 kg) tins.

3 Combine the flour and salt in a large mixing bowl and leave in a warm place. Crumble the fresh yeast (or granules) into a smaller bowl with the sugar, and add about ¾ pint (450 ml) water, warmed to blood heat. Leave for 10 minutes in a warm place, by which time the yeast mixture will be frothing.

4 Pour the yeast mixture on to the warmed flour, mixing with your hands. Continue adding the rest of the water (warmed to blood heat) until you have a dough. It will be considerably wetter than a white bread dough; don't worry, simply mix it with your hands until it comes away from the sides of the bowl. Don't knead it, but cover it with a piece of clingfilm, and put it in a warm place to rise for 30 minutes.

5 Divide the dough into two and knead each piece gently on a floured surface. (Don't overknead the dough, or it will become heavy.)

6 Shape the dough to fit the tins and leave for 10 minutes before baking in a very hot oven for 25–30 minutes. Tip the loaves out of their tins and cook upside down for a further 10 minutes.

7   When the bread comes out of the oven leave it to cool on wire trays so that it doesn't become soggy.

SPRING ONION ROLLS

Gibbons are a real favourite with the people from south Wales, just as scallions are much loved by the Northern Irish and spring onions by the British in general. And of course they are all the same thing, a distant relation to the leek.
This recipe for rolls from Lynda Kettle can easily be adapted to make loaves or, as she has suggested, shaped into the Chelsea Bun style. Lynda's skill for baking is something I really admire, and – as some people say – I agree that good bakers are born not made.

MAKES ENOUGH FOR 4

3 lb (1.5 kg) wholemeal flour	4 oz (100 g) gibbons or spring onions,
1 teaspoon salt	chopped green and white parts
2 oz (50 g) easy-blend dried yeast or 1 oz	1 tablespoon parsley, chopped
(25 g) fresh yeast	1½ pints (900 ml) warm water
½ teaspoon brown sugar	1 oz (25 g) butter

1   Pre-heat the oven to gas mark 7, 425°F (220°C).

2   Combine the flour and salt in a large mixing bowl and leave in a warm place for about 10 minutes. Sprinkle in the yeast and sugar and stir well. (Fresh yeast must be mixed with a little water first.)

3   Pour in the water and mix to a firm dough. Knead by hand or machine for 5 minutes.

4   Roll or pull the dough into a large rectangular shape, 2 ft (60 cm) long by 1 ft (30 cm) wide. Sprinkle over the gibbons and parsley and roll up from the long sides like a swiss roll.

5   With a sharp knife cut the dough into sections or buns and stand them up on end.

6   Butter a baking sheet and place the buns fairly close together, so that they will touch when risen. Leave them to prove in a warm place for 30 minutes.

7   Brush the tops with milk and bake for 15 minutes in a hot oven.

BEVERAGES

Anyone who has travelled through Wales will understand how many isolated rural communities were completely cut off in the past during the hard winter months. Self-sufficiency and a fair amount of sharing amongst neighbours would help to eke out food supplies and it was natural to stock up before the winter set in.

Home-made beverages were made by almost every household, whether it was ginger or dandelion beer, mead from local honey or wines made from every possible ingredient.

During the booming dairy industry in west Wales earlier this century, it was said that the Welsh preferred to drink cow's milk to beer, but there is little truth in that today!

Felinfoel Brewery is situated in a small village adjoining Llanelli, famous at one time for its tinplate industry and now for its rugby club. Both these activities encourage a great thirst, so it is no wonder that a small family brewing business should thrive!

Proud to have been the first brewery in Great Britain to introduce canned beers, Felinfoel was allowed to ship its beer to the front-line forces in the Great War to keep their spirits up. One of the present employees can remember her mother sending out cans to her father in the trenches.

When all beers are made by the same method and incorporate the same ingredients, why do they taste so different? A hard question to answer, but John Keddes, head brewer at Felinfoel, is a local man and although he has done painstaking research into other beers he can honestly say that no other brew suits him quite so well as his own!

Home-made wines have been part of country living in Wales for centuries, using traditional ingredients taken from the hedgerows. But when the Romans built their sophisticated fortresses in south Wales they weren't content with simple country wines so they planted grape vines. Over the past couple of decades some small vineyards have sprung up on south-facing slopes and some of the hardier French and German grapes have flourished. Martin Rogers has six acres of vineyards, and the potential for another 50 on his farm in Tintern and produces about 3500–4000 bottles of Tintern Parva wine per acre of fully fruiting vines. Having started only 10 years ago, Martin is still experimenting with vines and has planted Muller Thurgau, Reichensteiner, Bacchus, Ortega, Pinot Noir and Seyval Blanc.

Think of mead and think of historic Wales. Can't you just imagine King Arthur with a goblet of mead, and before him Welsh bards and Druids? Metheglin is a lesser-known drink, but equally famous in Wales. Based on honey, it combines the flavours of herbs as well and was popular with the royal court during the reign of Queen Elizabeth I.

Mead is still made in Wales today and one of the experts is Dinah Sweet. She has kept bees for 15 years, with 10 hives on Caerphilly mountain and another 10 in Whitchurch, Cardiff. After three years of bee-keeping, she decided to try her hand at mead. Now an authority, she helps other keen apiarists perfect their brew!

When researching into drinking traditions in Wales, Dinah discovered that honey was once used to sweeten ale instead of sugar, and she has successfully revived a recipe for Melomel, a wonderful concoction of honey and fresh fruit.

GORSE FLOWER WINE

Antoinette Hughes teaches home economics at the Agricultural College at Llandwnda near Caernarfon. With an Italian mother and an upbringing set firmly in the Welsh countryside, it is no wonder that Antoinette has a natural talent for making good country wines. Throughout the year she varies her recipe to suit whatever berries, blossoms or fruit are in season.
Either gorse or elderflowers can be used for this recipe; pick them early in the morning from a pollution-free area and remember to remove all the stems from the flowers.
If you haven't made wine before follow the basic steps from a wine-makers' guide book and adapt the ingredients to suit this recipe.

MAKES 1 GALLON

1 pint (600 ml) gorse flowers or
elderflowers, freshly picked
8 oz (225 g) raisins, chopped, or ½ pint
(300 ml) grape concentrate
2 bananas, mashed
the rind and juice of 3 oranges or lemons
2–2½ lb (1–1.25 kg) sugar
1 gallon (4.5 litres) boiling water

pectic enzyme
2 Camden tablets, crushed
sauternes yeast, yeast nutrient (available
from good chemist)
12 mg vitamin B
1 teaspoon grape tannin
1 teaspoon glycerine, optional – this gives
the wine a pleasant smoothness and
slight sweetness

1   Put the gorse flowers, raisins, bananas, lemon rind and juice and half the sugar into a large bowl or clean bucket. Pour on the boiling water, stir and leave to cool. Add the pectic enzyme and crushed Camden tablets, stir again and leave, covered, for 24 hours.

2   Activate the yeast, as per packet, and add to the must together with the yeast nutrient, vitamin B, grape tannin and glycerine if used. Stir, cover and leave to ferment on the pulp for 4–5 days.

3   Strain into a gallon demijohn and fit an airlock. Keep in a warm, dark place.

4   Dissolve the remaining sugar in 1 pint (600 ml) of water and bring to the boil. Cool. Add this sugar syrup gradually over the next couple of months.

5   When fermentation has stopped and the wine has cleared, rack the wine. Bung the neck.

6   Leave to mature for 2 months before racking again.

MEAD

The Welsh have a fondness for mead and, alas, it is said that their defeat and slaughter at the Battle of Catraeth was attributable to the excessive quantities of mead they drank beforehand.
This is rather an extravagant recipe with the price of honey today, but those who keep bees or perhaps have a yearning to unearth flavours from Wales's past, should have a go at this!
Dinah Sweet, who gave me this recipe, suggests that mead is probably best if kept three years before drinking – so don't delay, start right away!

MAKES ABOUT 1 GALLON

Equipment:
bucket
1 gallon container
airlock
siphon tube
funnel
filter paper
wine bottles
(Always sterilise equipment with Camden tablets.)

Camden tablets
3½ lb (1.5 kg) honey
7 pints (4 litres) water
tannin (or a brew-up of old tea-leaves)
1 teaspoon citric acid or lemon juice
1 teaspoon malic acid or apple juice
1 teaspoon tartaric acid or pear juice
yeast – wine or baker's
yeast nutrient

With cold water:
Put a Camden tablet in honey-and-water mix, and leave for 24 hours. Filter into a gallon container and add all other ingredients. The yeast should start to work within 3–4 days.

With hot water:
Boil the honey with 2 pints (1.2 litres) of water. Simmer for 10 minutes, removing waxy scum with a spoon. Allow to cool until temperature is blood heat, then filter into a gallon container and add the remaining water and other ingredients. The yeast should start to work within 48 hours.

Racking (for both methods):
As soon as the mead is clear (usually after 6 months), siphon off the clear liquid into another demijohn; as it clears again, repeat procedure and bottle. A Camden tablet should be added at each stage. Mead should be kept at a constant warm temperature to aid fermentation.

ROSE HIP SYRUP

Rose hips contain four times as much vitamin C as blackcurrant juice and 20 times as much as oranges. So this autumn, pick up your basket and go gathering. The best rose hips for cooking are the plump ones from varieties of Rosa Rubiginosa. Home-made Rose Hip Syrup is so much more delicious than the bought kind; delicious taken as a drink with hot water, or poured over a sponge pudding, ice cream or a bowl of plain yoghurt.

MAKES 1 PINT

8 oz (225 g) rose hips
¾ pint (450 ml) water
8 oz (225 g) sugar

1   Cut each hip in half with a sharp knife.

2   Put the water in a pan with the sugar and boil gently until the sugar has melted; then put in the rose hips. Half cover the pan and cook gently for 1 hour, adding more boiling water from time to time as needed.

3   Pour the liquid through a sieve, pressing the pulp with the back of a spoon, then leave to cool. You should have 7–10 fl oz (200–300 ml) of syrup.

4   Store in sterilised bottles.

DAMSON LIQUEUR

Living on an isolated farm in rural Wales, with few modern facilities, one would want to be well prepared to face the long, cold, dark winter. It might be wise to spend time in the autumn gathering the natural harvest from the hills and hedgerows and bottling fresh flavours to enjoy later on. And the prospect of a Welsh winter would be so much more appealing with a bottle or two of Damson Liqueur to see you through!

damsons
granulated or raw cane sugar
gin or vodka

1   Prepare the fruit by washing it well, removing stalks and discarding any blemished or over-soft damsons.

132

2   Sterilise a large needle over a naked flame and use it to prick the damsons all over.

3   Weigh the fruit and measure out an equal quantity of sugar. Put the prepared damsons in a suitable wide-necked sealable jar so that they fill it to the top – don't press them down, though.

4   Sprinkle in the sugar and fill the jar completely with gin or vodka. Screw on the top and shake the jar well.

5   Now comes the hardest part: leave the jar, unopened, for at least 3 months! Shake or turn the jar over twice a week.

ELDERFLOWER CORDIAL

This delicious Elderflower Cordial is similar in taste to Margaret Rees' Elderflower Champagne. Why not gather some bunches of elderflower from the hedgerows during the early summer, when the pretty white blossom smells quite musty? Using this simple recipe you can make enough cordial to last through the winter – and it will keep for a year or two. With its sunny yellow colour and marvellous heady flavour, the strength of the elderflowers gives the cordial a fragrant, almost exotic appeal. My neighbour, Non Henderson, who gave me this recipe, likes to drink the cordial mixed with some sparkling Welsh water and ice, and we both agree that it goes well with a little gin!

MAKES ABOUT 3 PINTS

2½ oz (65 g) citric acid	2 lemons, sliced (optional)
4 lb (1.75 kg) sugar	20 heads of elderflower
2½ pints (1.5 litres) water	¼ Camden tablet

1   Put the citric acid and sugar in a saucepan with a little of the water and heat gently to dissolve.

2   Bring the rest of the water to the boil, pour it over the lemons, if used, and elderflowers and add the sugar and citric acid solution.

3   Cover and leave in a cool place for 5 days, stirring well morning and night.

6   Stir in the Camden tablet to sterilise the cordial and strain the cordial into clean dry bottles. Store in a cool place.

DANDELION BEER

Dandelion beer, like ginger beer, was a popular drink with workers in the Welsh iron foundries and tinplate works. It was refreshing and thirst-quenching without of course being alcoholic.

MAKES 1 GALLON

8 oz (225 g) young dandelion plants	*1 gallon (4.5 litres) water*
½ oz (15 g) root ginger	*1 lb (450 g) demerara sugar*
1 lemon, rind and juice	*1 oz (25 g) cream of tartar*
	1 oz (25 g) yeast

1 Wash the plants and remove the hairy roots without breaking the main tap roots. Put them into a pan with the bruised ginger root, the lemon rind (no white pith) and the water. Boil for 10 minutes, then strain out the solids and pour the liquid over the sugar and cream of tartar in the fermenting vessel.

2 Stir until the sugar is dissolved. When the liquid is lukewarm, add the yeast and the lemon juice and leave the vessel, covered with a folded cloth, in a warm room for 5 days.

3 Strain out all the sediment and bottle in screw-topped cider or beer bottles.

4 This beer is ready to drink in about a week, when it hisses as the stopper is loosened. It does not keep very long.

5 Test the bottles daily to see that they don't get too fizzy. Even after only two days in the bottles it tastes smashing!

INDEX